Be Prepared

A Practical Handbook for New Dads

Gary Greenberg and Jeannie Hayden

Simon & Schuster Paperbacks
New York   London   Toronto   Sydney

Simon & Schuster Paperbacks
Rockefeller Center
1230 Avenue of the Americas
New York, NY 10020

First Simon & Schuster paperback edition 2004

SIMON & SCHUSTER PAPERBACKS and colophon are registered trademarks of
Simon & Schuster, Inc.

For information about special discounts for bulk purchases,
please contact Simon & Schuster Special Sales at 1-800-456-6798
or business@simonandschuster.com.

Designed and illustrated by Jeannie Hayden

Manufactured in the United States of America

50 49 48 47 46 45 44 43

Library of Congress Cataloging-in-Publication Data

Greenberg, Gary.
  Be prepared : a practical handbook for new dads / Gary Greenberg and
  Jeannie Hayden.
    p. cm.
  Includes index.
    1. Fatherhood. 2. Fathers. 3. Father and child. I. Hayden, Jeannie. II. Title.

  HQ756.G7 2004
  306.874'2—dc22

                                                        2004045156

ISBN 13: 978-0-7432-5154-9
ISBN 10:   0-7432-5154-7

This book is dedicated to our grandparents, William and Anna Barkin, Morris and Esther Greenberg, Margaret Hayden, Fran Hille, and Daniel and Johanna White. We're better parents and better people because of your warmth, generosity, and unshakable sense of humor.

Contents

INTRODUCTION

Congratulations, and welcome to the brotherhood of fatherhood.

For thousands of years dads have roamed the earth, hunting, gathering, trudging through the fields day after day in order to provide for their families any way they could. But it wasn't until the last quarter of a century that dads began to put down their spears and take an active role in the day-to-day duties of raising a child. So if women seem more natural at bringing up babies, it's only because they've had a huge head start.

The truth is that all those centuries of hunting gave men a skill set perfectly suited to new fatherhood. Patience, cunning, stamina, and on-the-spot improvisation play a major role in both stalking prey and baby raising. And much like a beast of the field, a baby is a very unpredictable creature, prone to wild mood swings and cranky tirades.

But raw skills alone don't make a great dad. Being prepared is the key—knowing how to handle every possible SNABU (Situation Normal All Babied Up) that can arise in a given day, and being able to implement Plans B and C when Plan A falls flat. A prepared dad can venture out into the world with the wind in his face and the baby strapped to his back, confident in the knowledge that he is ready for anything. The goal of this book is to foster that confidence.

Within these pages you'll learn tactics essential to keeping your little squirt healthy and happy and you and your partner mentally stable. Some of the procedures may seem a bit strange at first, but rest assured: everything in this book has been thoroughly researched, dad-tested, and baby-approved. Furthermore, everything in the book has been approved by several distinguished fellows of the American Academy of Pediatrics.

At its heart, *Be Prepared* is a how-to manual. It's not the kind of book that gets emotional and touchy-feely about the father-baby relationship. And although we freely admit that sharing your baby's first year is one of the most exciting, life-affirming experiences you'll ever have, we also know that you've got a lot to learn in a short amount of time. So we'll stick to the nuts and bolts, and leave the sentiment to you.

Now hoist up your diaper bag and get moving.

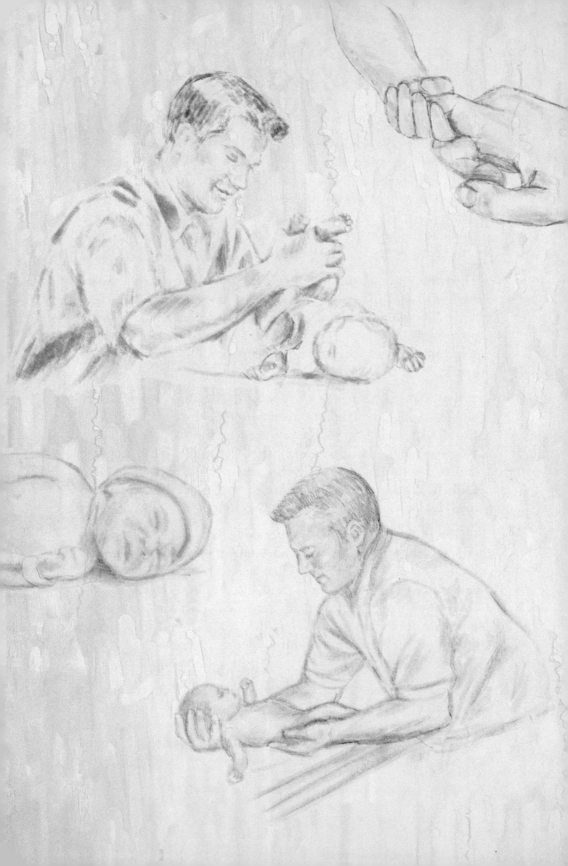

THE FIRST WEEK

What Your Newborn
WON'T Look Like

The picture here is what a lot of dads imagine their newborns will look like: a big, healthy, well-formed miniature version of themselves. But this is actually a picture of a three-month-old. Fresh-out-of-the-womb newborns look very different. As a matter of fact, your newborn may not bear any resemblance to you, your partner, or any known members of your species.

To familiarize yourself with a newborn's physical appearance, carefully study the picture on the following page. That way you won't be in for any surprises come delivery day. And since you'll get a good view of the baby as it's coming out, and your partner will not, she'll probably be taking her cues from the look on your face. The last thing you want to do is freak her out for no reason.

5

What Your Newborn
WILL Look Like

puffy, bloodshot eyes

cone-shaped head from squeezing through the womb

giant head measures a whopping 1/4 of baby's overall length

lanugo—fuzzy hair on face, back, and shoulders. This will eventually disappear.

flat nose and off-center chin from womb pressure

vernix caseosa—a cheesy substance that protects baby's skin in the womb

genitals may be swollen but will eventually shrink back down

skinny, structurally unsound legs

whiteheads, blotches, birthmarks, bruises, and rashes are all common newborn skin conditions and will eventually disappear

NEWBORN Party Tricks

REFLEX	confirmed	try again later
	✓	
Rooting		
Moro		
Palmar		
Plantar		
Stepping		
Avoidance		

Let's face it: when you're spending time with your newborn, you've got to find ways to make your own fun. Conducting a field test of his reflexes is a perfect way to do just that. You'll come away with a greater appreciation of his skills, and you'll have some cool party tricks to pull out at the next family gathering.

Though he looks helpless, your newborn comes pre-programmed with a complete set of reflexes that help him search for and secure food, avoid danger, and extricate himself from sticky situations. Now if you could just get him to change his own diaper.

Here are some of the more common reflexes and ways to test for them:

Rooting Reflex

Stimulus: Stroke the baby's cheek.

Response: He will turn his head toward the sensation.

Explanation: This helps the baby find the breast or bottle.

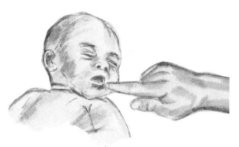

Moro Reflex

Stimulus: Give your baby the sensation of falling or make a sudden loud noise.

Response: He'll throw his arms and legs out.

Explanation: Helps him to gain his balance or to signal for help.

Palmar (Hand) and Plantar (Foot) Grasp Reflexes

Stimulus: Stroke the palm of the baby's hand and the bottom of his foot.

Response: The baby will grasp your finger with his hand and will curl his toes down toward your finger.

Explanation: This helps the baby to reach and grasp objects with his hands. The plantar reflex is an evolutionary hold-over from the days when we had to hold on to our mothers' fur.

Newborns have such a strong grip that they can hang from a bar, but don't try this at home.

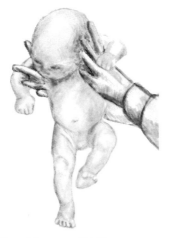

Stepping Reflex

Stimulus: Holding the baby under both arms, stand him up (supporting his head with your fingers) and place his feet on a flat surface.

Response: He'll lift one leg and then the other, simulating a march.

Explanation: This is either a precursor to walking or a way for the baby to kick objects away.

Avoidance Reflex

Stimulus: With the baby lying down, move an object toward his face.

Response: The baby will turn his head from side to side, close his eyes, and try to get out of the way.

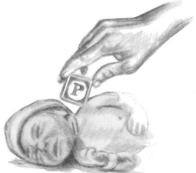

Explanation: Self-defense. (Prepares him for dodgeball.)

Most reflexes usually disappear after several months, either evolving into a conscious act or completely disappearing.

Handing Over the BABY

**VISITORS MUST
-WASH HANDS-**

Before
Touching
Newborn

Upon seeing your new baby, your friends and family members will likely fall into two categories—the smotherers and the deserters. The smotherers will engulf the baby with affection, and the deserters will make a bee-line for the farthest corner of the room.

Provided they're healthy, it's a good idea to let close friends and family hold the baby. You'll get a few moments of freedom, and you can secretly audition potential babysitters in the process.

Moreover, holding a new baby is a rite of passage that brings these people closer to you. You're showing them that you trust them with the heir to your throne, and they won't forget it.

But before you hand over the baby, here are some things to keep in mind:

- All holders need to wash their hands. Viruses such as colds are transferred through physical contact. So if anyone shakes hands with a cold sufferer and then touches your baby, you'll find yourself standing in the shower at 3 a.m. trying to decongest his sinuses.

- Tell them to relax. Babies, like wild animals, have the ability to pick up on nerves, so the less tense the holder is, the better chance the baby will feel comfortable.

- If you or the receiver are at all uncomfortable, have them sit down and cross their arms above their lap (see below), and gently place the baby in the crook of their arm. Make sure they support the head. This position is particularly good for children.

 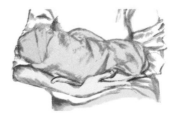

DENYING ACCESS

There are always some people who will ask to hold the baby, and you, for whatever reason, don't feel comfortable letting them. It might be the look in their eyes, the liquor on their breath, or the polyester of their jumpsuit. This is one place where you should probably trust your instincts, and you can use the excuses below to stop them dead in their tracks:

"The pediatrician warned us that his rash is very contagious."

"The baby is allergic to deodorant/detergent/hair spray."

"He just got his shots and is very irritable."

"He is afraid of people with beards/glasses/nose rings/curly hair."

"He has projectile diarrhea, and I don't want to pay your dry-cleaning bill."

YOU ARE the A.V. Club

Being a dad, you're expected
to have an innate knowledge of
electronic gadgetry. Whether you're an
A.V. geek or a confirmed technophobe, the job of documenting
your baby's first year will likely fall into your hands.

DIGITAL CAMERAS

If you haven't gone out and bought a digital camera by now, what are you waiting for? The prices are dropping and the quality keeps getting better. And for a new dad with a lot on your plate, bringing film in for processing and picking it up is valuable time that could be spent napping.

Downloading is the way to go. You can crop, resize, adjust colors, and then print out your favorites. And what better way to torture your friends and family than with daily photo e-mails of your ever-changing progeny?

Buy a camera that's high in megapixels (image quality) but small enough to take anywhere. Also purchase a memory card (your reusable "film") that holds at least 50 high-resolution images. Since babies are uncooperative by nature (those gurgles are his way of saying "No paparazzi!"), it may take ten tries to get one usable shot.

It is strongly recommended that you purchase, power up, and test all of the features of your camera at least a month before your partner's due date. You don't want to be desperately clawing at the battery door as the baby's crowning.

Three Tips for Taking Great Baby Shots

Add variety. No matter how cute your baby is, nobody wants to sit through 20 shots of him lying on a blanket. To make the photo-viewing experience more palatable, you've got to add interest. Dress him in festive mismatching outfits, have different family members try to imitate his face while holding him, surround him with garden gnomes or army men, put him on a big serving tray, anything to make the shot more dynamic.

Always shoot at the highest resolution. You never know when you're going to capture that perfect image for the holiday card, and you don't want it to look all grainy.

Use the self-timer. Twenty years from now you're going to want your child to know that you once had hair. So set the camera on a tripod, stump, or stroller, activate the self-timer, and get into a few shots. Just because you are the family archivist doesn't mean you aren't archivable. (That being said, it's also a good idea to teach your partner how to use the camera.)

CAMCORDERS

Video is the perfect medium with which to capture your nipper's development. Each piece of video you shoot is a time capsule for that particular stage of his physical, emotional, and verbal progression. And you just can't get the full effect of spit-up running down your partner's neck with a still camera.

If you don't own a digital camcorder, you might want to consider buying one. Digital offers superior image and sound, and there's no loss of quality in transfers. And most important, you can download the video to your computer and edit out the long, boring parts before showing it to anyone else. Keep in mind that the average guy can stomach about five minutes of baby video, so edit with extreme prejudice.

Two important features to consider are size and durability. Make sure the camera will fit comfortably in one hand, and that you can easily access the record button and zoom toggle. To research durability, call your neighborhood electronics repair shop and ask which camcorder models they see the least. Chances are you are going to drop the camera at some point, and you don't want a model that self-destructs on impact.

Your buddies will all be enthralled by your new baby.

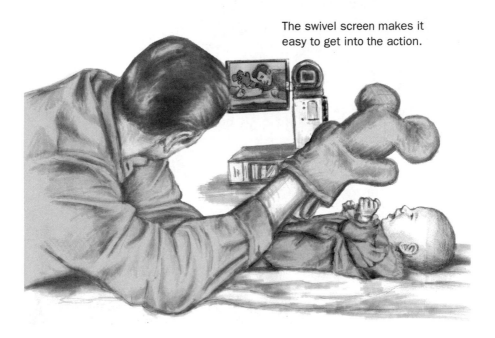

The swivel screen makes it easy to get into the action.

Tips for Taking Great Baby Video

Don't save taping for birthdays and holidays. Everyday moments are often the most compelling. Watching a baby knock over a tower of blocks is more exciting than watching his baptism.

Get into the action. Put the camera down, rotate the LCD screen 180 degrees, and hit record. This way you can see exactly what the camera is capturing, and how much you can move before you go out of frame.

Have an extra battery on hand. LCD screens tend to suck up power, so an extra fully charged battery means that you'll never have to cut your video session short.

Get down and dirty. Shooting a baby from your head height is really unflattering to him. It makes him look even shorter, smaller, and squatter than he already is. You also get a distorted view of his face. For best results, lie down on your stomach and shoot him at eye level.

Why Your Partner May Not Be FUNCTIONING Properly

Your partner's body has just been through the biological equivalent of a train wreck, and she may spend much of these first weeks collapsed on the couch, your bed, the tub, the floor—basically, anyplace that can provide momentary relief. She may not comb

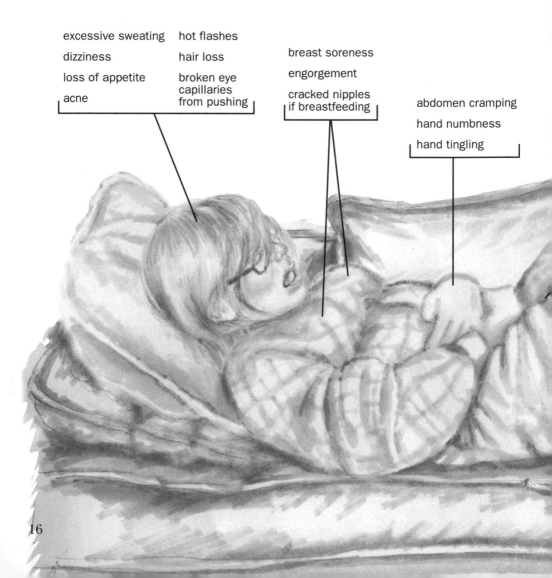

excessive sweating

dizziness

loss of appetite

acne

hot flashes

hair loss

broken eye capillaries from pushing

breast soreness

engorgement

cracked nipples if breastfeeding

abdomen cramping

hand numbness

hand tingling

her hair, brush her teeth, or change clothes for days on end, spending most of her time in your baggiest shirts and sweatpants.

But have no fear. If the healing goes smoothly, she'll be shedding those sweats and resuming personal hygiene by around three weeks A.B. (after birth).

Below you'll find some of the more common birth-related afflictions.

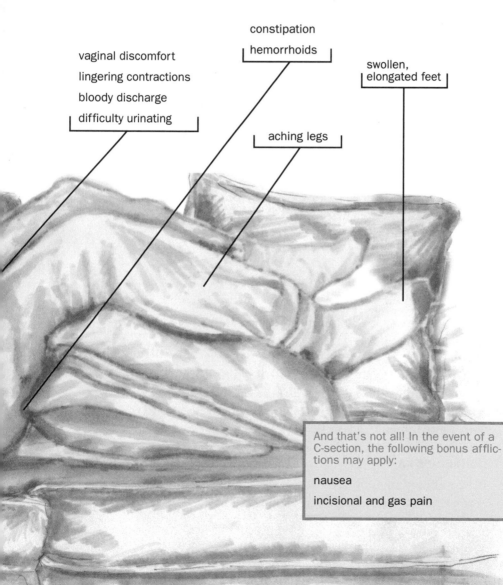

constipation

hemorrhoids

vaginal discomfort

lingering contractions

bloody discharge

difficulty urinating

swollen, elongated feet

aching legs

And that's not all! In the event of a C-section, the following bonus afflictions may apply:

nausea

incisional and gas pain

BREAST vs. BOTTLE

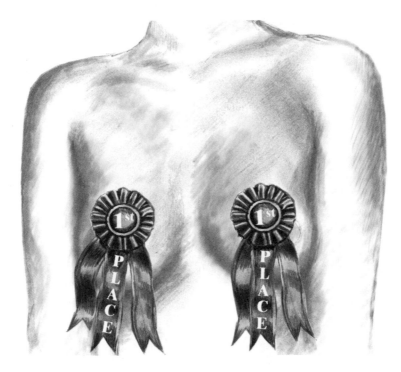

Should you choose to feed the baby breast milk or formula? This age-old question may be best elucidated through a head-to-head, topic-by-topic, no-holds-barred comparison.

Nutrition   Winner: **Breast milk**

As a nutritional product, breast milk is without equal. Not only does it contain antibodies that protect against disease and allergies and other valuable enzymes, but it actually adapts to the baby's nutritional needs as he grows. It's almost spooky.

Convenience   Winner: **Breast milk**

Breast milk is the ultimate fast food. It's pre-packaged, pre-heated, and best of all, nobody can screw up your order.

Cost   Winner (by knockout): **Breast milk**

Unless your partner is charging by the quart, breast milk wins this
one easily. Also, breastfed babies spit up less, cutting down on your
dry-cleaning bills.

Smell   Winner: **Breast milk**

The diapers of breastfed babies don't have much of a smell at all.
This is thought to be a biological adaptation to keep away preda-
tors. So if you live anywhere near wild dingos, definitely opt for
breastfeeding.

Mother's Birth Recovery   Winner: **Breast milk**

Nursing helps her uterus shrink back to its original size (sorry you
had to read that) and helps her shed excess pregnancy weight
(but aren't you glad you read it till the end?).

Mother's Stress Level   Winner: **Formula**

Breastfeeding moms have a lot to deal with—pain from feedings
and milk production, exhaustion from grabbing sleep in two-hour
increments, and constant worries about the baby getting enough
to eat. It's a tough row to hoe, and she'll need your support.

Results:
Breast 5, Bottle 1

Conclusion: If your partner
is able to breastfeed, it's
probably a good idea to do
so. If not, don't worry.
Almost everyone born in
the 1950s through the
1970s was formula-fed, and
now these people are
running our country! On
second thought, you
should do whatever you
possibly can to breastfeed.

Bidding Farewell
to the BREAST

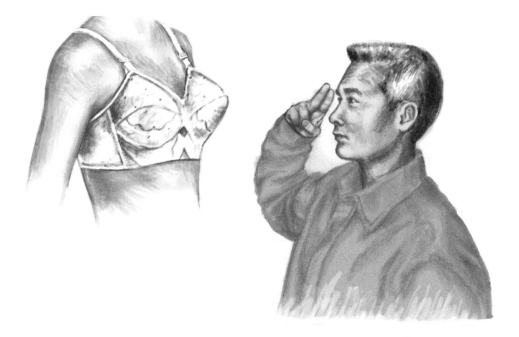

From the moment your partner starts nursing, her breasts are off-limits to you. The property rights have officially transferred to the baby. At some point you may be offered a time-share opportunity, but in the meanwhile, just go about your business and disregard the parade of mammaries flouncing by your face day and night. And don't even consider the irony that at the very moment they become forbidden, her breasts are bigger and firmer than they've ever been before (and will ever be again).

Watching your partner breastfeed can trigger a double jealousy. You're jealous of the baby for his all-access pass to your partner's body, and you're jealous of your partner because she can instantly soothe and feed him by offering the breast, while you've got to jump through hoops to quiet him down.

But just because your body doesn't produce a beverage doesn't mean you're off the hook on the breastfeeding front. Studies have shown that a father's help and support is a key factor in how long and effectively a mother breastfeeds.

Be prepared to help out by:

- sterilizing and assembling breast pump parts,

- running for hot compresses in the event of a clogged duct,

- presiding over one of her night feedings so that she can remain in bed, semi-conscious throughout.

To take over a night feeding, bring the baby to the breast, help him latch on, switch from one breast to the other, burp him, change him, and put him back to sleep. Your partner will appreciate the effort, and it may help you secure that time-share.

And after the first month, you can—and should demand to—feed him his first bottle. This is a profoundly enjoyable experience, followed by another joyous moment, his first bottle burp, which is usually fuller and deeper than a breast burp (on account of the air bubbles).

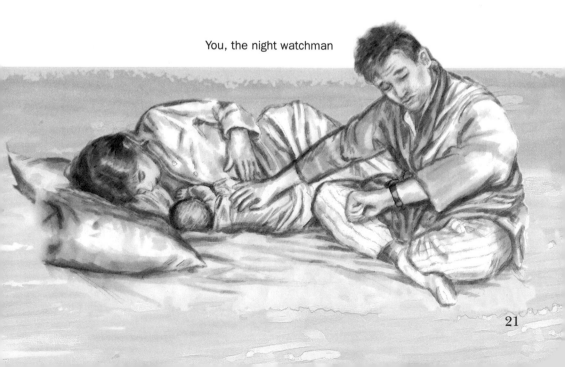

You, the night watchman

The Joy of BURPING

Burping a baby is a great task for a dad because, unlike most early baby care, it is results-oriented. You perform a specific series of maneuvers and almost always get a pay-off. And when you hear that magical rumble, you can't help but think, "He's one of mine."

There are three methods of burping, each one designed for the baby to spit up on a different part of your clothing. This is why you need a burp cloth, or in some cases, a burp tarp. If you're wearing something decent, it's best to give yourself as much coverage as possible.

Method A

The baby's head is resting on your shoulder and your arm is under his bottom. Use your other arm to gently rub or pat his back.

Method B

Sit the baby on your lap facing out. Lean him slightly forward as you hold his chest and chin in one hand and burp with the other. Be sure to support his head.

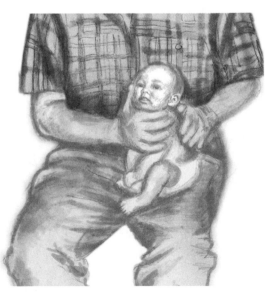

Method C

Lay the baby face-down across your lap with his head resting on one knee and his stomach on the other. Hold his bottom with one hand and burp with the other.

Once your baby can support his own head, you can use the following technique to get out the really stubborn gas bubbles. Sit the baby on your lap, hold him in both hands, and roll his body slowly from side to side and around and around before burping. This may help the air bubbles rise to the surface and result in less spit-up. Make sure not to tilt him too far to one side or the other.

It's a good idea to burp twice during a feeding, mid-meal and post-meal. The mid-meal burp will give the baby room for the second course.

The Basic CHANGE

Since you'll be changing more than 2,500 diapers over the next year, it's worth learning proper changing technique. Sloppy procedure can result in leakage, rash, or contamination of your clothes and the surrounding area.

For insurance, place a clean diaper under the soiled one.

Place finger between baby's ankles to keep them from rubbing together.

Make sure diaper is not too tight.

Supplies You'll Need:

A clean diaper

Wipes and a washcloth

A changing table or other smooth, flat, clean surface on which to place the baby

Procedure:

1. Lift the baby's legs off the table using the ankle hold (thumb around one leg, forefinger between the legs, and the rest of fingers around other leg).
2. Place a clean diaper under the dirty one, just in case the baby decides to let loose mid-change.
3. Unfasten the tabs of the dirty diaper and stick them back onto themselves, as you don't want them to stick to the baby.
4. Using the ankle hold, remove the diaper, revealing the clean one underneath. Wipe the baby thoroughly. For boys, immediately put a washcloth over the crotch to prevent squirts. For girls, wipe front to back, to prevent vaginal infection.
5. Fold the bottom of the new diaper up between the baby's legs and fasten both sides using the tabs. If you can't fit two fingers between the baby's skin and the diaper, then it's too tight.

Never leave the baby unattended on the changing table.

Your Newborn and Your PET

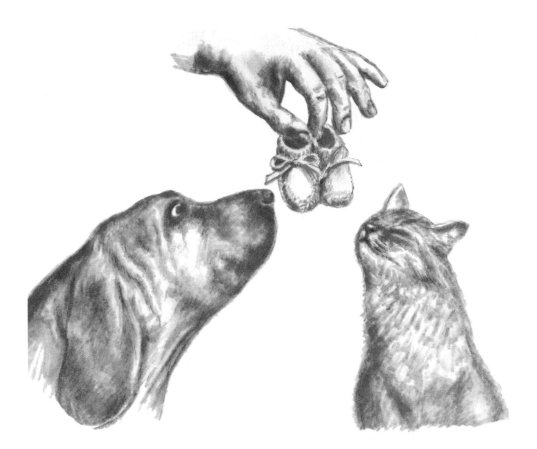

DOGS

Your dog sees the world a bit differently than you do. To him, you are the alpha male, your partner is the alpha female, and the three of you are a pack. Upon arrival of the baby, your dog may experience several weeks of post-partum depression. But if all goes smoothly, your new baby will soon be accepted as a junior alpha, eligible for all the benefits of membership—protection, loyalty, and relentless face-licking.

Before the Baby Arrives

- Dogs learn by association, and you don't want your dog to associate the baby with negative things such as diminished play time, being kicked out of the bedroom, and the relocation of his food dish. If you are going to implement changes, it's important to do so at least a month before the baby arrives.

- Play a recording of a crying baby to get the dog used to the loud, high-pitched screams. Dogs have a keen sense of hearing, and may panic upon first listen, but eventually they adjust. It can help to desensitize you as well. You can download a three-minute audio crying jag from www.beprepared.net.

- Some dog experts suggest that several months before the due date, you "play pretend" with a doll to acclimate the dog to the new family dynamic. The dog watches you change, feed, sing to, and put the doll to sleep. This is certainly an option, but it may be easier and less humiliating to get a friend to bring their baby over to your house once in a while.

- Make sure your dog understands the "Down!" "Stay!" and "Drop it!" commands, and if not, train him. Also, take him to the vet to make sure his shots are up-to-date and that he's parasite-free, and secure someone to take care of him while you're at the hospital issuing the "Breathe!" command.

Post-Partum

- Soon after the birth, take a piece of clothing that the baby has worn and bring it to your dog so that he can scent-bond.

- Upon arrival from the hospital, your partner should greet the dog first while you hold the baby. Your partner hasn't been home in a while, and the dog's natural excitement may give way to jumping and rough-housing. When all is calm, put a leash on the dog and let him view the baby from ten feet away. Then slowly bring the two closer to one another. If the dog remains calm, allow him to sniff the baby.

- Don't let the dog lick your baby's face for the first few months. The baby's immune system is still immature, and your dog's tongue has been to places you'd rather not think about.

- Even the most gentle dogs shouldn't be left alone with the baby. Always be quick to reprimand aggressive behavior and reward good behavior.

If all goes well, your baby and your dog will become inseparable.

A mesh crib tent can inadvertently turn your baby's crib into a bunk bed.

CATS

Almost all of the dog-based suggestions will work with cats, although you might not have much luck with the commands. Because cats are instinctually drawn to moving objects, they are generally disinterested in newborns. That being said, it's never a good idea to leave the two alone in a room together.

Cats have a tendency to curl up against warm bodies and may try to get in the crib with your sleeping baby, which is a bad idea, as the cat could inadvertently scratch, bite, or possibly smother the baby. Here are two ways to make sure the cat stays out of the crib:

- After you put the crib in place (several months before the due date), put something on top of the mattress that is really unpleasant for the cat to touch. Cut a piece of cardboard the size of the crib mattress, cover it with double-stick tape, and place it in the crib, so their paws become sticky. Or cover the mattress with tinfoil (they hate the crinkly sound). After one or two ill-fated encounters, the cat should leave the crib alone.

- Purchase a mesh crib tent that fits snugly over the crib to deny access. The cat may end up hanging out on top of the tent, becoming a living mobile.

How to Entertain
a NEWBORN

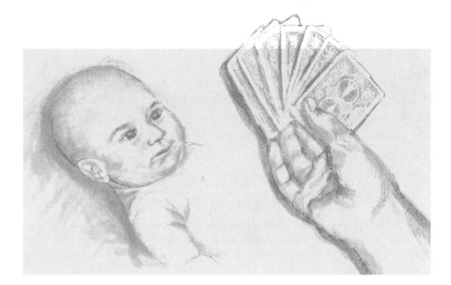

One of the best—and only—ways to play with your newborn is through stimulus-response games, where you present him with various objects or sensations and wait for a reaction. And, yes—staring blankly is considered a reaction.

The following games focus on sensory development:

Vision

Newborns' eyes can focus best on objects ten to twelve inches away from their faces, and they can't see colors.

Clubs and Spades

Get a deck of cards, separate out the clubs and spades, and hold them in front of your baby's face. Slowly fan them out, bring them back in, and fan them out again. Show him a royal flush and see if his poker face holds.

Hearing

Hearing is fully developed in newborns, and they seem to prefer high-pitched voices to low ones, which is presumably why people use baby talk.

Sound Tracking

On one side of the baby, crinkle a bag, shake a can of nuts, and jingle your keys until he turns his head to the sound, then do the same on the other side.

Touch

Touch is the first sense that starts developing in the womb, and by birth is well developed. Some areas are more responsive than others, with the palms of the hands, the bottoms of the feet, and the area around the mouth being the most sensitive.

The Texture Buffet

Gently rub different areas of your baby's skin with objects of varying textures. You can use a clean damp sponge, a silk tie, the fur lining of a glove, and a bicycle pump to blow air on him.

Smell

Newborns have a keen sense of smell, and within the first couple of days show a distinct preference for the scent of their mothers' milk.

Fridge Inventory

Take a bunch of odoriferous foods out of the fridge—cheese, onions, pickles, and fish are good choices—and hold them up to your newborn's nose. Wait for a reaction. If you aren't sure if the yogurt has gone bad, maybe his face will give you the answer.

Taste

Your baby's taste buds began developing in the womb, and he now will show a distinct preference for sweet tastes rather than sour ones. But seeing as babies can't have anything but breast milk or formula for around six months, you'll have to curb your impulse to have him suck on a lemon wedge.

THE FACIAL RECOGNITION TEST

Show the baby the three faces on this page. See how he gravitates toward the recognizable face? This preference for faces is genetically built in and helps the newborn bond with his parents. And if by chance your baby prefers one of the other faces, you just may have a budding Picasso on your hands.

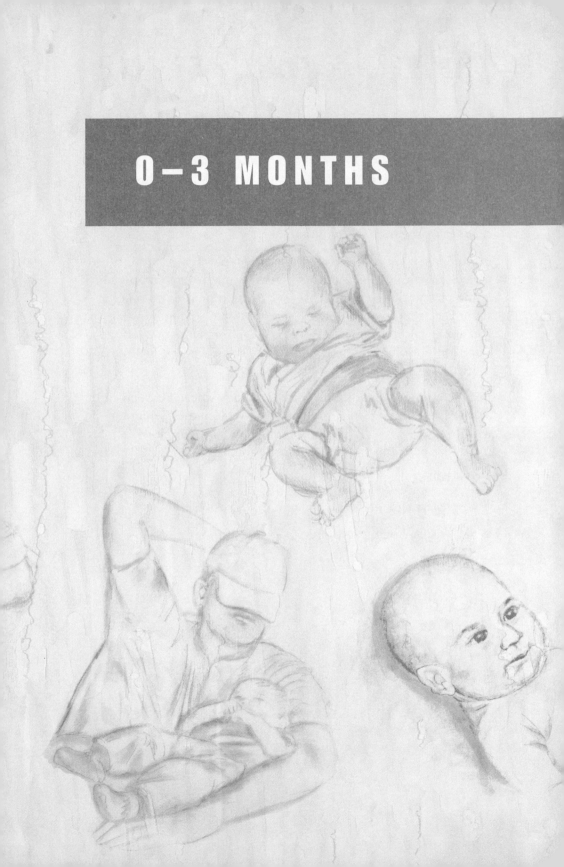

0-3 MONTHS

The First-Month SLUMP

Fatherhood can hit you like a sucker punch. The baby arrives, you're showered with help and gifts and food for a week or two, and then everyone leaves. And you are suddenly hit by this overwhelming feeling that nothing will ever be the same again. Someone has taken away your old life and replaced it with this really long, frustrating community service project.

For the first couple of weeks post-baby, you may feel anxious, depressed, and lonely, and why shouldn't you? You're completely at the mercy of a relentless little dictator, and there is no relief in sight. But as you're wallowing, it's important to remember that you are not alone. Fathers the world over, from Copenhagen to Cape Town, from captains of industry to ditch diggers, have all gone through this rough patch.

For the majority of dads, this phase lasts somewhere between eight and twelve weeks, at which point you switch into the "I might as well make the best of it" phase. Several factors combine to help lift the dark clouds from your head, including:

- The baby is sleeping longer hours.

- You're feeling more adept at handling and troubleshooting her.

- She's finally smiling at you (the baby, not your partner).

If this period lasts more than three months, or you begin to feel completely overwhelmed or withdrawn, talk to your partner and friends and think about seeking professional help.

Moms and Mood SWINGS

Dad beware! If you thought that your partner's PMS was difficult to deal with, then you'd better brace yourself for the wrath of PPMS (Post-Partum Mood Swings). Affecting three out of four new moms, this condition is often referred to as the Post-Partum Blues or Baby Blues, but the word "blues" does not do it justice.

Plainly speaking, your partner will be all over the map, so expect the unexpected. One minute she'll scream at you for putting on a diaper incorrectly and the next minute she'll accuse you of not helping out. She may banish you to the basement, then criticize you for not being romantic. Try to think of it as your penance for not having gone through labor.

Keep in mind that much of this behavior is beyond her control. Right after the birth, her hormone levels are bouncing around like Ping-Pong balls, playing havoc with her brain chemistry. So

when you see her throwing breast pump parts across the living room, remember to cut her some slack.

PPMS can last anywhere from a couple of days to a month or more. It can be really tough on a dad, especially since you're trying to adjust to the baby as well. But since taking a room at the Best Western is not an option, you've got to do what you can to help see her through this rough patch.

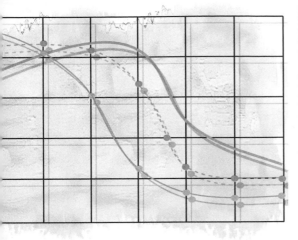

Employing these four policies will make things easier on both of you:

Policy #1: Ears Open, Mouth Closed

Guys tend to be fixers by nature. You see a problem, and you find the solution. Of course it's logical, but in this case it may backfire. Your partner may need comfort, not a ten-point plan of action.

Policy #2: Strike It from the Record

Think of all of the belligerent things that you've said after four or five beers. Now consider that she's under the influence of chemicals far more mind-altering than Budweiser. Six months from now, she may not even remember some of the names that she called you. (You should write them down though, just in case.)

Policy #3: Be an Army of One

Don't expect much from your partner these first weeks. You may need to do everything short of breastfeeding, so be prepared to carry the load. Enlist the help of relatives and order plenty of take-out.

Policy #4: Take Her Out

Isolation is a big contributor to PPMS, so the sooner she gets a change of scenery, the quicker she may come around. Remember that newborns are very portable, so grab her and the baby and take a stroll around the block. The exercise will help her get back into shape, and it releases endorphins that can lighten her mood.

Post-Partum Depression

This condition is far more serious than PPMS and affects about 10% of new moms. If your partner's emotional state is seriously impeding her ability to function, or her symptoms last longer than a month, suggest that she consult her obstetrician. If she resists, you can bring up the fact that her condition is very treatable, and that every day she waits is one less day she'll be able to enjoy the tot.

Scrubbing Your Sprout

Bathing a baby is a mission that requires a steady hand and nerves of steel, which is why it's a perfect challenge for a new dad.

For a segment of the population that just lounges around all day, newborns get surprisingly dirty. That fresh newborn scent can quickly give way to the odor of curdled milk if your baby's been left unwashed for too long. Bathe her every other day, or as much as seems necessary, but if her skin starts to dry out, you'll have to cut back.

Don't give the bath until the umbilical stump falls off and, if you've got a boy, the circumcision has healed. Before then just sponge your baby down.

Bathing Equipment Checklist

❑ A baby tub or other bathing apparatus

❑ A large plastic bucket

❑ A plastic cup

❑ Baby soap and shampoo

❑ Two or three washcloths

❑ A dry, folded towel next to the tub in which to wrap baby upon completion

Where to Do the Deed

When deciding where to scrub your sprout, take into consideration safety, your comfort, the baby's comfort, and proximity to a water source.

In a baby tub placed in the sink

Many tubs dock right into the sink bay, anchoring it into place. Also, having the baby at this height will give you good leverage, and you'll be right next to a water source. Just make sure that you point the faucet away from the baby at all times.

On the floor

Nervous parents sometimes place the tub on the floor for the first couple of baths, until they are confident that they won't drop the baby. Make sure you put some garbage bags under the staging area, and use a pillow under your knees.

In a baby tub inside the big tub

This can be a bit hard on the back, but the baby is low to the ground, and it won't matter if water goes everywhere.

With you in the big tub

Some babies find the baby tub confining, and would prefer your company. The big tub offers both of these options, but it's not recommended until you get comfortable with the bath-time ritual.

Bathing Procedure

1. Pour warm water into the tub and bucket. The water should be nice and warm, but not hot. Test it with your elbow. If it feels hot to you, then it's definitely too hot for the baby. You only need 3–4 inches in the tub.

2. Undress the baby and place her in the tub. To keep her from becoming cold and whiny, lay a washcloth across her chest and keep pouring warm water from the bucket over her. But always have one hand holding her in place.

3. Using a clean washcloth, wipe the eyes from the bridge of the nose out. Then move on to the rest of the face, outer ears, and neck. The baby's neck folds are surprisingly cavernous, providing ample storage space for dirt, lint, fermenting spit-up, and maybe even spare change. If left unwashed, they can become infected.

4. Move onto the arms, legs, and torso. The armpits, belly button, and leg folds are also perfect nooks for dirt and grime to gather. Use soap on the body a few times a week, and just water the rest of the time, but you can soap the diaper area every time. Rinse off the soap with cups of clean water from the bucket.

5. Wash the hair. Because babies lose much of their heat through their heads, do this last. Use a couple of drops of baby shampoo several times a week.

6. Place the baby on the towel and pat her dry.

A large, printable version of the Bathing Procedure list is available at www.beprepared.net. Tape it to the wall next to the bathing location for reference.

Keeping shampoo out of the eyes

To avoid getting shampoo in her eyes, use one of the following tactics:

- Place a dry washcloth over her eyes as you pour water from the bucket onto her head; or

- Swaddle the baby (see pg. 51) so that only her head sticks out. Then hold her over the tub with her back on your forearm, her legs tucked inside your elbow, and her head and neck supported by your wrist and hand. This is called the football hold. Tip her head down so that when you rinse her with the bucket water, it will drip down into the tub and not into her eyes.

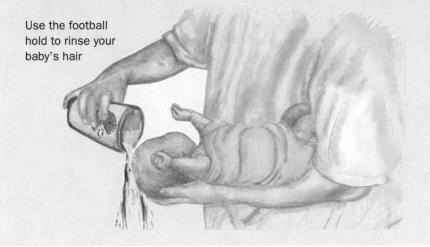

Use the football hold to rinse your baby's hair

Cradle Cap

When you are washing your baby's hair, you may notice big scaly flakes on her scalp. This is called cradle cap, a common and harmless newborn condition that doesn't seem to cause any discomfort and usually disappears by about three months, just in time for the day care prom. To get rid of the scales, you can massage the scalp with mineral oil or petroleum jelly, remembering to be gentle around the fontanels (the soft spots on the top of her head). You can also use a soft toothbrush to clean her scalp, and avoid putting hats on her when indoors, because sweat can exacerbate the condition.

GRIPPING A SLIPPERY BABY

The Sock Glove

A clean cotton sweat sock can stick to a baby's skin better than your bare hands. Cut out a thumbhole so you can maintain hand functionality.

The Armpit Hold

Use this hold for any situation in which the baby could possibly slip down in the tub. Lay the baby's head on your forearm, your wrist supporting her neck. Encircle her upper arm with your thumb and fingers.

Accidents Will Happen

At some point your baby will poop in the tub. Maybe it's a defense mechanism, like a squid inking. It's a disgusting and frustrating occurrence, but it's one of those parental rites of passage that officially confirm you as a dad.

In order to decontaminate the tub, you'll need to:

- pull the baby out, wrap her in the towel, and place her on a secure surface,

- quickly drain the tub, rinse it out with soap and water, and then refill it,

- get another clean towel for post-bath wrapping, put the baby back in, and start over.

As far as urine in the tub goes, most new dads don't change the water, for these reasons:

- It's really hard to tell if a baby has peed in the tub.

- Urine is mostly water anyway.

- Most dads have relieved themselves in the shower for all these years, and their feet have never fallen off.

The Diving Reflex

At some point or another you may accidentally lose your grip and the baby's head will go underwater for a second or two. Don't panic. Newborns come equipped with something called the Diving Reflex, an automatic response that prevents them from breathing in water should they go under. In the few seconds it would take you to pull your baby back up, chances are great there would be no harm done to her. This reflex lasts for a few months and then disappears.

Obviously you shouldn't take this as a cue to become lax about tub safety.

USEFUL BATHING CONTRAPTIONS

Contoured bath pad

This pad cradles your baby and elevates her head above the water. The pad is placed in your bathtub, and absorbs bath water to keep the baby warm. A popular model is called *The Safer Bather*.

Baby bath tub with sling attachment

The sling cradles the newborn so she won't slip around while bathing. And it converts to a regular baby tub when she outgrows the sling.

The EZ Bather

A very simple device consisting of fabric covering a sloped frame. The fabric holds the baby in place and keeps her head above the water. You can place it in the sink, a baby bath tub, or a regular bath tub, and it disassembles, making it very portable.

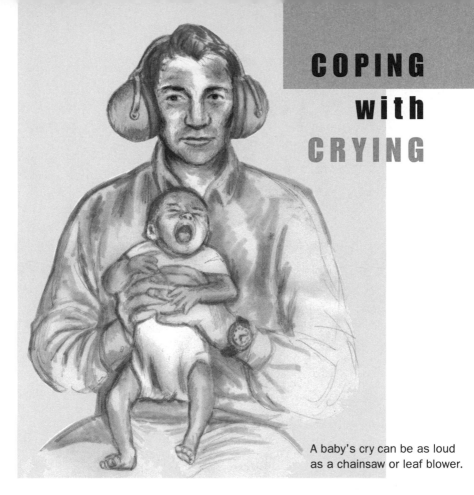

COPING
with
CRYING

A baby's cry can be as loud as a chainsaw or leaf blower.

If you have the misfortune of working for a tireless, demanding boss, we've got bad news for you: now you've got two of them. And the baby is undoubtedly the less forgiving of the two. But then again, you'll never be able to calm down your other boss by blowing a raspberry on his stomach.

If you are skeptical about the baby's absolute power over you, then try to spend thirty seconds NOT responding to her cries. The sound of a baby's cry triggers a biological "alarm reaction" that:

- raises your blood pressure,
- increases your circulation,
- elevates oxygen levels to your brain.

So the baby's Pavlov, and you're the dog. And on top of that, the human ear is most sensitive to sounds at 3 KHz, almost the exact central frequency of a baby's cries.

Discomfort
Fatigue   Pain
Hunger   Colic
Boredom

IDENTIFYING THE SIX CRIES

Be prepared to spend approximately 500 hours of your baby's first year listening to her cry, give or take a wail or two. If you'd like to be on the low end of this curve, you'll need to be able to figure out what she needs at any given moment. That's why you'll need to learn how to identify the six baby cries.

Like the CIA code breakers of World War II, you've got to use your powers of decryption to break through your tot's seemingly random wails. Listen to her cadence, tone, pitch, and volume. Mark it in your memory, and then respond. Does a bottle quiet her? If so, you've discovered the hungry cry. If not, try one of the many other maneuvers described on the following pages. With time, you'll become cry-lingual.

Not every baby cries exactly the same way, but there are six basic crying patterns that are common among babies worldwide.

Hunger

A pattern of low-pitched, rhythmic moans, growing more and more insistent. Short cry, pause, louder cry, pause, even louder cry.

Fatigue

A soft, breathy blubbering. If you listen closely, you may hear vibrato. The cry is often accompanied by eye rubbing.

Pain

A high-pitched cry that comes out of nowhere. It's as if somebody triggered a car alarm.

Discomfort

A consistent pattern of forceful sobs, which can break into a full-scale wail if not attended to. Discomfort cries are usually about being too hot or too cold, an uncomfortable body position, or a soiled diaper.

Boredom

A low-volume whimper that stops and starts irregularly. It doesn't sound frantic and usually disappears as soon as you enter the room.

Colic

A burst of urgent high-pitched scream-ing that can go on for hours. Each wail can last for four or five seconds, taking the baby's breath away. A lengthy pause follows while the baby catches her wind, then it starts all over again.

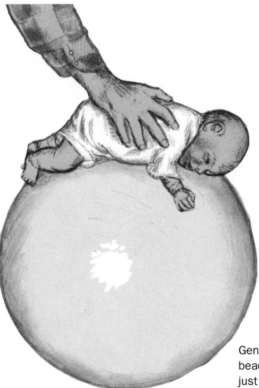

Gently rocking your baby on a beach ball or an exercise ball just might cure what ails her.

HARDCORE SOOTHING TACTICS

What happens when you've tried all of the obvious soothers and yet she's still sobbing uncontrollably? It's time to break out some alternative tactics. Rest assured the methods below have been proven effective; they just aren't as well known as the classics. For instance, the baby-on-the-ball idea wasn't discovered until a resourceful dad, whose arms were falling asleep from holding his screaming daughter, decided to rest her on a nearby exercise ball. He began gently rolling the ball around and around, his hand firmly on her back. She miraculously quieted, and lo and behold, a soothing tactic was born.

If one method doesn't work for you, move on to another. But don't cross any of them off your list, because what works today might not work tomorrow, and vice versa.

Gas Relief

Gas bubbles can cause havoc in the newborn digestive system.

- Lay the baby on her back and bicycle her legs back and forth or bring both knees up to her chest and back down and repeat. This pressure on the stomach frequently causes a gas expulsion.

- Go into your home office and sit down on your swivel chair. Place the baby facedown on your lap, and swivel the chair back and forth while gently patting her back.

- Try using gripe water or colic drops, all-natural over-the-counter potions designed to reduce infant gas. And if your partner is breastfeeding, suggest she avoid gassy foods like beans, cabbage, and broccoli. Tell her that you and the baby will both appreciate it.

Change of Scenery

Giving the scamp a new perspective may calm her down.

- Hold her in front of a mirror. She may be mesmerized by the new kid, or your reflected face watching her.

- Climbing up and down stairs with her in your arms combines interesting visuals with exciting motion. Or you can put her in the stroller and roam up and down the hallway. Or try driving around the block a couple of times.

- Don't be too proud to pass the baton to your partner. The baby may respond to her new smell, voice, and touch, and you'll get some time to decompress, at least until she returns the favor.

Startling

If you startle a crying baby, sometimes she will forget why she was crying in the first place. But once the crying stops, be prepared to quickly segue into another activity.

- Turn off the lights, wait a few seconds, and then turn them on again. Repeat if necessary.

- Place a baby's hand or foot under running water (but test the water temp first).

- Imitate the baby's cry right back to her. She may stop to watch. Whispering might also force her to listen. Or try animal noises.

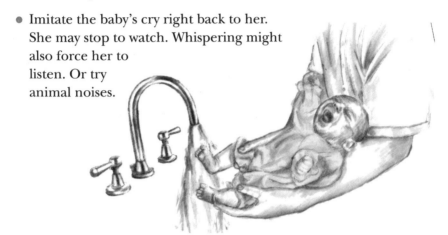

Re-creating the Womb

Some babies long for their former residence. Try any one or a combination of these techniques:

- Put her in the car seat carrier, grab the handle, and gently swing her back and forth. This can approximate the closeness and motion she felt in the womb. You can also buy an electronic swing to replicate this movement.

- Many babies suck their fingers in the womb. You can either use a pacifier or let the baby suck on your freshly washed pinky finger. Make sure the finger is palm side up so it won't scratch the roof of her mouth.

- A warm bath with white noise in the background can help her regain the feeling of being enveloped.

- Immobilize her with a swaddle.

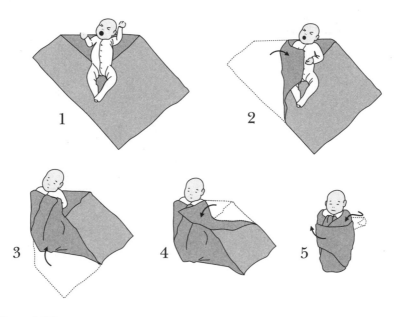

Swaddling

Swaddling mimics the closeness of the womb. Though many babies are comforted by this miniature straitjacket, others would rather not revisit the womb experience, thank you, and will quickly tell you so.

Follow the step-by-step instructions below. A square blanket may hold better than a rectangular one, but either can be used.

1. Lay a receiving blanket on a flat surface, and fold one corner down about six to eight inches. Then lay the baby down so her head is directly above the folded corner.

2. Take the left corner of the blanket and pull it across her body, tucking it in below her back.

3. Fold the bottom of the blanket up to the baby's chest and tuck it into the first fold.

4. Take the right corner and pull it across her body and behind her back.

5. If you have enough blanket, you can tuck the right corner into the fold beneath the back of the baby's neck.

If your baby prefers having her arms free, you can try a modified swaddle by repeating the above steps with both the left and right sides tucked in under her arms.

BRACING FOR
UNHAPPY HOUR

During these months most babies become extremely edgy toward the end of the day, sometimes crying for an hour or more. This fussy period is believed to be the baby's way of rebooting her nervous system. Some time between 5:00 and 8:00 p.m., a baby's brain hits maximum capacity and goes into cry mode.

If you're a working dad, unhappy hour can be particularly miserable because just as you open the door, the baby freaks out. It could start to give you a complex.

And as a guy, you may feel that it's your duty to troubleshoot the kid and come up with a solution. When all of your best efforts go unrewarded, anxiety and frustration may set in, bringing you one step closer to putting that "Baby for Sale" ad in the classifieds.

But here are three facts that might make you feel better:

- Unhappy hour affects more than 75% of all babies.

- This pattern should stop at around twelve weeks.

- Letting the baby cry in her crib for a couple of minutes in between comforting attempts won't traumatize her, and just may be a welcome break for the both of you.

In the meantime, get a pair of earplugs to dampen the noise level, which can get up to about 100 decibels, about the same volume as a chainsaw or leaf blower.

COMBATING COLIC

It comes suddenly and without warning. It wreaks havoc for approximately eight weeks, and then abruptly disappears, leaving a trail of frayed nerves and empty aspirin bottles in its wake. It's colic, and it may be coming to your town.

The term "colic" refers to prolonged periods of crying, usually several hours or more. No one knows exactly what causes colic, but many experts think that it's got something to do with the stomach.

Fortunately, there are ways to combat colic, which afflicts up to 20% of all infants. You can try some of the gas relief suggestions discussed previously, as well as the two additional methods below.

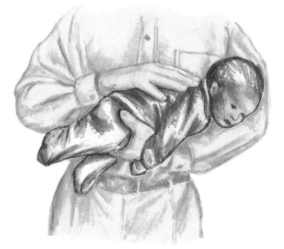

The Popeye Hold

1. Stand with your arm bent at the elbow and your palm facing upward.

2. Sit the baby on your palm, facing you.

3. Gently lay her down on your forearm, so her head rests on the inside of your elbow.

4. Rock her from side to side while stroking her back.

Your forearm is exerting gentle pressure on her abdomen, which, in combination with the rocking, may soothe her.

The Cry and Dry

1. Take a warm towel out of the clothes dryer and put a cool towel in. Turn the dryer on.

2. Sit on top of the moving dryer. Fold or roll up the warm towel and place it on your lap. (Make sure it's not too hot.)

3. Lay the baby on her belly across your lap so that her stomach rests directly on top of the towel. Hold her bottom with one hand and stroke her back with the other.

4. When the towel cools down, open the dryer and switch towels. Turn the dryer back on, fold the warm towel, and repeat step 3.

The combination of the heat, the vibration, the position, the noise, and your hands on the baby's back may prove too powerful for even the most stubborn case of colic.

The laundry room may become your second home for a while.

Wrestling the
BREAST PUMP

If you have an aversion to the breast pump, it's completely under-standable. After all, it's a bit unnerving watching a mechanical device mercilessly slurping at your partner's bare chest. You can't help but think, "If robots made pornography, this is what it would look like."

But soon you'll realize that the pump is your friend. Not only will it allow you to bottle-feed your baby, but you'll finally be able to get a sitter and go out on an actual date for once. And if your partner suffers from clogging or engorgement, pumping can provide the quickest relief.

There are two types of pumps—manual and electric. The manual pumps are inexpensive, light weight, and small, so your partner can use them at work or in transit. But the constant hand squeezing is both tiring and time-consuming, and because a hand pump can have up to ten parts, the constant drill of disassembling, sterilizing, and reassembling (most likely your job) gets old fast.

Electric pumps are fast, easy, and rigged for double-barrel pumping. You just have to figure out if you want to rent the hospital-grade tractor pull pump or purchase one of the portable consumer models. If your partner is trying to increase output, you'll want one with a powerful motor. Just remember that milk production, like old school capitalism, is based on supply and demand, so the more milk she pumps, the more she will produce.

c.

b.

a.

Basic Parts

There are several brands of electric pumps, each using a similar (but not interchangeable) set of parts.

A breast shield screwed on to a bottle (a) connects to a motor (c) by tubing (b).

The milk is pumped directly from the breast into the bottle. All the parts that come in contact with milk (basically, [a]) should be taken apart and rinsed after every feeding, and sterilized in boiling water before the first daily use. The tubing should be washed weekly, and whenever milk or condensation is visible. You dry the tubing by attaching it to the pump and turning it on for a minute or two.

Pump manufacturers claim that sharing a pump is unsanitary. But because pumps are expensive, many people borrow the motor and buy new tubing and shield/bottle assemblies.

If your partner has any problems with breastfeeding or pumping, you can contact your local lactation consultant (not a joke—they exist and are listed in the yellow pages) or La Leche League, an international breastfeeding organization.

STORING PUMPED MILK

Short-Term Storage—Detach the container from the pump, seal it up, and write the date on a piece of tape and stick it to the bottle. Milk can last five days in the fridge.

Long-Term Storage—You can purchase generic disposable bottle bags for easy milk storage. Or, as an alternative, you can pour the milk into clean, sterile ice cube trays, put the trays in freezer bags, and place them in the freezer. The milk will last at least two months. When you are ready to use it, pop an ice cube from the tray, put it in a plastic baggie, and heat it under warm water. When it's liquefied, transfer it to a bottle. Each cube equals approximately two ounces of milk.

Store breast milk in ice cube trays, but be sure to mark them so there won't be any surprises at your next party.

GLOSSARY OF BREASTFEEDING TERMS
That You Might As Well Know

Colostrum—Thick yellowish liquid secreted from the breasts during the first days after the baby is born before the breast milk comes in. Colostrum provides the baby vital nutrients and antibodies.

Engorgement—Common during the first weeks of breastfeeding, engorgement occurs when breasts are filled to capacity, often causing discomfort. Remedies include immediate feeding, pumping, and warm compresses.

Clogging—When a milk duct is blocked, a tender lump appears on the breast, and it may be painful. Remedies include emptying the breast regularly, massage, and warm compresses.

Rooting Reflex—A newborn's instinct to turn her head toward any stimulus that brushes her cheek. She may also open her mouth, stick her tongue out, and search for a nipple.

The Boppy Pillow—An unfortunately named horseshoe-shaped cushion that fits around the torso to support the baby's body during feedings. Later on, as the baby tries to sit up, you can put the pillow around her so she won't "bop" her head on the floor. It also becomes an entertaining headpiece.

The evolution of the Boppy Pillow

BOTTLES UP!

Giving your baby a bottle is your initiation into Total Provider status. It's comforting to know that if your partner were ever sucked into another dimension by aliens, you could still feed your baby until she reappeared.

And once the baby accepts the bottle from you, she'll most likely accept it from anybody, which means you can hire a babysitter so you and your partner can go out on the town for a couple of hours.

Some things to know before the first bottle feed:

- If your partner is nursing, introduce the bottle when the baby is around one month old. Any earlier and the little squirt may still be figuring out the breast, any later and she may be too set in her nursing ways.

- Don't be discouraged if she doesn't take to it immediately. Keep trying with different nipple shapes and sizes, and with milk at various temperatures. Almost all babies eventually catch on.

- Give the bottle once a day but not more. You don't want her to reject the breast.

- Administer these first feedings without your partner in the room. The baby may look at her and get confused. And your partner may start sobbing, seeing the bottle as an early symbol that your baby is leaving the nest.

Bottle-Feeding Procedure

1. Warm

Run the bottle under hot water. Never use a microwave, because it destroys enzymes in breast milk, and the milk heats unevenly.

2. Test Temperature

Squirt a few milk droplets onto the underside of your wrist. The bottle should be no hotter than body temperature.

3. Bait the Hook

Right before inserting, smear some milk around the outside of the nipple.

4. Commence Docking Maneuvers

Sit with the baby lying in the crook of your arm. Elevate her head. If you lie her flat, she is more susceptible to choking and ear infections. Activate the rooting reflex and insert the bottle.

5. Feed

To prevent gas pains, tilt the bottle at such an angle that milk completely fills the nipple. Never prop up the bottle and leave the baby alone during feedings. In the beginning, you may have to periodically remove the bottle to let her catch up.

6. Burp

Burp after every two ounces or whenever she gets fussy during feedings.

Preparing Formula

Even if you haven't noticed any strange mutations in the local fauna, it's a good idea to sterilize the water that you use in formula for the first three months by boiling it.

The easiest way to prepare formula is a six-pack at a time. Get a clean beer pitcher and mix in the correct ratio of formula to water (put the water in first to avoid clumping). Stir vigorously. Fill six empty bottles with the desired amount, put the caps on, and stick the bottles in a six-pack container. These bottles will remain usable for forty-eight hours.

Cleaning Bottle Parts

You only need to boil the bottle parts once, before the first use. After that, just wash with soap and warm water after each use, or you can save yourself some time and effort by cleaning all the parts in the top rack of the dishwasher, using store-bought dishwasher baskets for the nipples and rings.

Sleeping Like a BABY

NIGHT OF THE LIVING DAD
Showtimes at 9:15, 9:34, 11:20, 11:27, 12:53

When you hear the phrase "newborn sleep patterns," disregard the word "patterns." Unless you invoke chaos theory, you may not see a pattern at all, at least for the first month or so. Your baby may sleep for five minutes or five hours. And when she sleeps for five hours, try to resist the urge to break out the cigars, because chances are her next nap will last for exactly five minutes.

The devolution of the exhausted dad

This is a very surreal time for new dads, because your day is broken up into something like ten identical mini-days, coming at irregular intervals, consisting solely of feeding, burping, changing, and putting the baby back to sleep. Days and nights bleed into one another. You're not sure when you last showered or ate or brushed your teeth. After about a week of this, you develop the same look that you see on first-year medical residents.

SLEEP-INDUCEMENT METHODS

Singing Babies haven't heard enough music to know what's off-key, so you are off the hook. Choose droning, monotonous songs like "100 Bottles of Beer," and gradually get softer and slower as you see the baby starting to nod off.

Feeding All of that sucking must tire babies out. Many times you'll notice, mid-feed, this drunken look on your baby's face, and within seconds she'll be out.

Confinement Accustomed to the womb, many babies equate comfort with confinement, and they'll sleep better if you find ways to pin them down, either with a swaddle or by putting them to sleep in the car seat.

Motion Even before birth, your newborn fell into bad sleep habits. She was rocked to sleep in the womb by your partner's every movement, and now that she's on dry land, she will probably expect the same treatment. To keep her in perpetual motion, you can either go battery-powered, using the electronic swing or vibrating bouncy seat; gas-powered, taking the car out for long, slow trips around the block with her in the car seat; or dad-powered, walking around with the baby in the stroller or front carrier.

White Noise

White noise is an amazing sleep inducer.
Not only does it mask unwanted outside noises,
rendering the baby oblivious to ringing phones,
creaking doors, and barking dogs, but it also mimics the sound of
the rushing fluids and shifting body weight that your baby heard
in the womb. In one study, young babies were three times as likely
to fall asleep while listening to white noise as those not exposed.

Fortunately, you can create your own white noise using common
household appliances:

- Put a small household fan, air conditioner, or air purifier in the
  baby's room.

- Rip the antenna off an old boom box and turn the knob all the
  way to the right or left for twenty-four-hour commercial-free
  white noise.

- Briefly run the vacuum or hair dryer.

- Get a fish tank.

*The motors in vacuum cleaners and hair dryers tend to wear out
quickly, and you may not want to run a fan or AC in the middle of
winter. But you can download a five-minute track of white noise at
www.beprepared.net. Copy the sample as many times as it takes to fill up
a recordable CD. Then just stick your new disk into the player, hit repeat,
and you're good to go.*

For Those About to Rock

Two things to consider before you start rocking:

Pace Studies have shown that the most effective rocking mimics the mother's walking pattern, which is approximately sixty rocks a minute (rocking to the left and then to the right equals two rocks). This is a brisk pace compared to the slow, gentle rocking you might picture in your head, but let your baby be the judge. She'll let you know if you are going too fast.

Music Many babies are comforted by strong, methodical beats. Some parents use metronomes to put their babies to sleep, but in lieu of that, try reggae music. The beat is solid and steady, and it's got a natural buoyancy that will complement your rocking. And best of all, most reggae music cycles at around sixty to seventy beats per minute, tailor-made to your baby's needs. *(Bob Marley's "Buffalo Soldier" is almost a perfect sixty b.p.m.)*

No Baby, No Cry

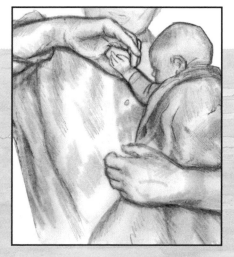

The Sleep Test

Before you lay the baby down, you've got to make sure that she's entered into a good, sound slumber. To test her level of sleepiness, lift one of her arms a couple of inches and then let it fall. If she offers any resistance, then you need to do some more rocking.

The Delicate Art of the Transfer

Transferring a sleeping baby to a crib or bed is like defusing a bomb. It's a painstakingly delicate process. One false move and you've bought yourself another half hour of rocking. To ensure a smooth transition, follow the steps below:

1. While rocking, gently reposition your hands so that you'll be able to pull them out from under her, spatula-like, when you finally put her down.

2. Walk her slowly toward the crib or bed, rocking continuously. As you walk, search the floor for toys or other objects that could serve as tripping hazards or audible land mines.

3. Once you are in front of the mattress, gradually let the rocking come to a halt.

4. Bend over the mattress as you lay her down on her back, keeping body contact the whole time. Chances are the mattress will be cold, and your warmth may be the only reason she isn't startled into wakefulness. Stay in this position for a minute or two.

5. As you pull away from her, slide your hands out from under her back and onto her chest. Keep them there for another minute.

6. Take a deep breath and gently remove your hands.

Baby Monitors

If you choose to put the baby in another room, it's a good idea to get a pair of baby monitors. Yes it's true that parents survived without them for thousands of years, but those parents didn't have a home theater with

DVD surround sound. Test out the monitors with your partner before the due date. Have her stand in the baby's proposed sleep space and whine while you walk around the house and listen.

And be aware that all monitors have inherent flaws. If one night you suddenly hear what sounds like your baby ordering a pizza, don't panic. Monitors pick up cordless phone interference, police radio transmissions, and other baby monitors in your neighborhood. Try switching the channel (most come with at least two options), and if that doesn't work, you might need to exchange it for another brand.

About SIDS Risks

Many parents spend a great deal of time worrying about SIDS (sudden infant death syndrome). But in truth, the risk is very, very low—less than 1 in 1,300, or .07%. And if you take these simple precautions, your risk will be even lower than that.

- Put the baby to sleep on her back.

- Use a firm mattress and a thin fitted sheet under the baby.

Since research into SIDS is ongoing, consult your pediatrician for the latest facts.

- Avoid overheating your baby.

- Keep stuffed animals, pillows, comforters, or heavy blankets out of the baby's sleep space. If you need a blanket, it's best to use the sleep sack wearable blanket (see pg. 84).

- Don't smoke, and keep the baby away from people who do.

- If possible, your partner should breastfeed.

- Take an infant CPR class.

"The Big H," a common family sleeping formation

YOUR BED, YOUR RULES

Do you want to share your bed with the baby? Some guys think it's great, and others feel that the bed is one of the last kid-free spaces left in the house and would prefer to keep it that way.

It's a bigger decision than you might think, because once the baby settles into your bunk, she's not likely to go back to the crib anytime soon. After all, now that she's used to The Hilton, do you think she's going to settle for Motel 6?

Here are some factors to think about:

Your Sleep Many infants grunt, moan, and wiggle in their sleep. This is because they spend a lot more time in R.E.M. dream sleep than adults, which is ironic, because they don't have nearly as much to dream about.

Your Partner's Sleep Your partner can breastfeed without having to get out of bed if the baby is next to her.

The Baby's Sleep The closer you are to the baby, the more likely you are to respond to every whimper, which may wake the baby up unnecessarily.

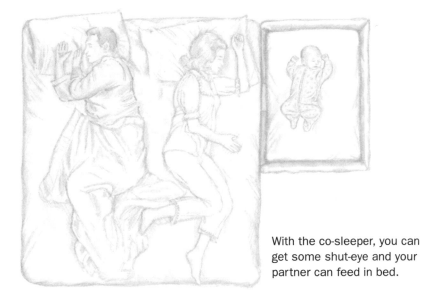

With the co-sleeper, you can get some shut-eye and your partner can feed in bed.

Safety If you are very heavy, an extremely deep sleeper, take sleeping pills, or drink to excess, you shouldn't have the baby in your bed. Even if you are none of the above, you've got to adhere to the previously mentioned SIDS specifications.

And soon you'll have to deal with a rolling baby, which may mean rails and other gadgets to keep her in place.

Sex When it's finally time to resume sex, a baby in your bed will force you to find other, more challenging places for your exploits.

Intangibles Many dads have said that there's no substitute for watching the baby wake up next to you, stretch out her arms and legs, and pass gas.

Hooking Up a Sidecar

If you want the baby reasonably close to you but not in the bed, you may want to hook up something called a co-sleeper. It's a three-walled mini-crib that hooks on to the side of your bed. Your partner can easily pull the baby into the bed for feedings, and push her back into the co-sleeper when finished. When the baby becomes able to move around, you can put the fourth wall up to keep her from rolling into your bed at will.

PLACES YOUR BABY CAN NOD OFF

Infants have a wide variety of sleep options, including the following apparatus:

Car seat — Some babies like the womb-like confinement of the car seat so much that they sleep there exclusively for the first six months.

Snuggle nest — A mini-bed that you put on top of your mattress, between you and your partner. It has little rails so the baby won't roll out. This probably won't work in anything less than a king-size bed.

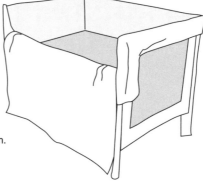

Baby carrier — Your natural walking motion can rock the baby to sleep in the front carrier or sling.

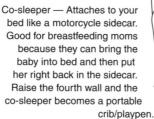

Co-sleeper — Attaches to your bed like a motorcycle sidecar. Good for breastfeeding moms because they can bring the baby into bed and then put her right back in the sidecar. Raise the fourth wall and the co-sleeper becomes a portable crib/playpen.

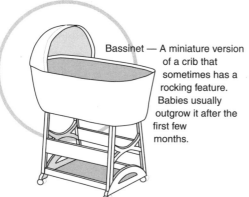

Bassinet — A miniature version of a crib that sometimes has a rocking feature. Babies usually outgrow it after the first few months.

Changing pad — Some people put this on the floor for naps, and babies are held in place by the lipped edges.

Vibrating bouncy seat — The steady vibrations soothe baby to sleep, but there's not much padding, so it may not be as comfortable as other options.

Automatic swing — This device has a hypnotizing effect on babies. Just remember to have a fresh set of batteries on hand.

Crib — You can turn your baby's crib into a CRIB by purchasing accessories that will soothe her to sleep and entertain her when she wakes up. These attachments include mobiles, activity centers, and attachable toys.

Stroller —When you fold the seat all the way back and go for a walk, the baby can sleep in the stroller for hours.

Dresser drawer— In a pinch, you can form a makeshift bassinet by lining the inside of a sturdy drawer with firm, safe padding.

Returning to WORK

Sometime during these months you'll most likely be punching out of baby world and back into work world. If you've taken advantage of the Family Medical Leave Act, you can take up to twelve weeks of unpaid leave or arrange to work a temporary part-time schedule. Either way, your employer can't penalize you for taking time off to be with the baby. Some companies, however, are exempt from the FMLA, so make sure you're covered before barging into your boss's office and demanding your rights.

For more info about the FMLA, go to www.beprepared.net.

SLEEP DEPRIVATION AT WORK

Exhaustion is by far the biggest obstacle you'll be facing as you try to reinsert yourself into the working world. You'll be doing the same tasks you used to, but they'll take twice as long. You'll read the same page three different times before comprehension kicks in. The basic rules of division and multiplication suddenly elude you. And forget about giving a presentation. The right words are always just out of reach.

Studies have shown that your I.Q. actually drops with each hour of sleep lost. Your language center starts to shut down, your memory becomes sluggish, your reaction time slows, and you become irritable. The good news is that lack of sleep can't kill you (unless you are operating heavy machinery).

There are ways to fight the effects of sleep deprivation. It's been proven that naps, even short catnaps, can do wonders for your mental agility. Researchers from NASA found that airline pilots who napped for an average of 26 minutes improved their performance by 34%. (Presumably they weren't napping on the job.)

At home, naps were acceptable. But unless you've got your own private office, you're going to have to find more innovative ways to catch some shut-eye. Here are three possibilities:

- On your lunch hour, you can always go to your car, adjust your seat as far back as it can go, and drift off.

- If your company has a gym, you can lie down on a mat and do some deep relaxation exercises.

- If you're really desperate, go into a stall in the men's room, take a seat, prop a clean roll of toilet paper under your neck like a violin, and shut your eyes.

STAYING UPRIGHT AT YOUR DESK

There are times when a nap is not an option, and you've just got to slog through the day somehow. Here are some tactics for keeping conscious in your cubicle. Four or five of them, used in conjunction, just might do the trick.

1. An oscillating fan for a cool, irregular breeze

2. Post-it notes for everything (because you can't trust your brain)

3. Coffee (which dehydrates) and a sports drink (to replenish your electrolytes)

4. Chewing gum (preferably peppermint or cinnamon, as they are natural stimulants)

5. Sharp, dissonant music (bagpipes are perfect)

6. Hourly breaks to climb stairs (which will oxygenate your blood)

7. Energy bars for lunch (a heavy meal will tire you)

8. A tray of cold water for your bare feet (a bit preposterous, but it works like a charm)

9. A prominent display of baby photos to remind people to cut you some slack in case you actually do keel over onto your keyboard

Reading SPORTS ILLUSTRATED to Your Baby

Experts agree that reading to even very young babies is a good idea. They say that hearing words read aloud helps to "map" a baby's brain to focus on, and eventually recognize, certain sound patterns, the building blocks of language. It's basically "Hooked on Phonics" for the newborn set.

Why not institute a daily dad-baby reading ritual as soon as possible? It'll be fun for the both of you, and although she can't tell a duck from a doorknob, hearing your voice will strengthen her connection to you and give her comfort.

As for reading material, you can never go wrong with *Sports Illustrated.* Why *S.I.*? For the following reasons:

- Baby will be attracted to the pictures. Most of the uniforms have a lot of contrast, which babies respond to visually. They LOVE the umps.

- Baby will be enthralled by your play-by-play commentary. You can even try a Howard Cosell or Marv Albert voice if you're feeling it.

- Baby will be fascinated with your over-enunciations of the names of famous athletes (DI-KEM-BE MO-TUM-BO, HI-DE-KI MAT-SU-I, and half of the NHL).

- You'll get the lowdown on all the games you are no longer able to watch, keeping you in touch with at least some vestige of your former life.

- The excitement you show about your subject will rub off on the baby. And if sports is not your bag, you can always read the L. L. Bean catalog, *Wired, Cat Fancy,* etc. Stay away from *Maxim,* though. It may trigger the breastfeeding impulse.

A Guy's Guide
to STROLLERS

Guys who don't go stroller shopping are missing out on a golden opportunity to throw around phrases like "turning radius," "spring-action collapsibility," and "off-road performance." And if you leave the task to your partner's sole discretion, then you can't gripe when you find yourself trudging through the mall pushing an antique pram with a teddy bear–printed canopy.

Three things you should do before buying any stroller:

Test Drive

Assess maneuverability and performance in tight corners. Can you steer it effectively with one hand? Are the handles high enough so that you aren't hunched over? Turn an aisle of the store into a slalom course where you can test its limits.

Inspect Moving Parts

Collapse and expand the unit. Can you do it with one hand (assuming the baby will be in the other)? Test the locking mechanism, reclining mechanism, and brakes. Are they well made? User-friendly? Is there a five-point safety harness? Shake the stroller to determine sturdiness.

Lift and Carry

Would you be able to carry it up a flight of stairs? Would your partner be able to hoist it into the trunk? Remember that you're also going to be hauling diapers, wipes, toys, bottles, and up to 25 pounds of baby.

Some misguided parents think it's a good idea to "let the baby choose," by putting her in various strollers to see how she reacts. This is a very bad idea, mostly because babies cry for many different reasons, and what you think is a stroller rejection may be a hunger pang.

THE SIX BASIC STROLLER TYPES

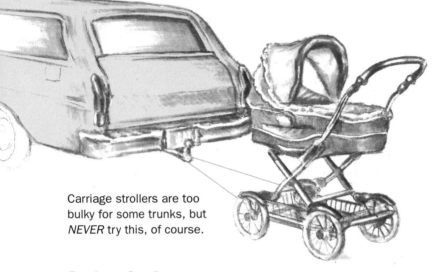

Carriage strollers are too bulky for some trunks, but *NEVER* try this, of course.

Carriage Combos are traditional baby carriages that morph into strollers when the baby outgrows the carriage. Since babies under three months should be lying flat (for head support), carriages provide an ideal setting for the newborn. And the carriage configuration enables the parent and baby to face one another. But when you unclamp the carriage top and snap on the stroller seat, they don't function nearly as well. The carriage chassis is heavy, and the wheels don't swivel, so maneuverability is limited.

Stroller Combos are similar in concept to the carriage combos. The difference is all in the chassis. They weigh considerably less (usually between 20 and 25 pounds), fold up compactly, and feature wheels that swivel 360 degrees, making them better in tight spaces.

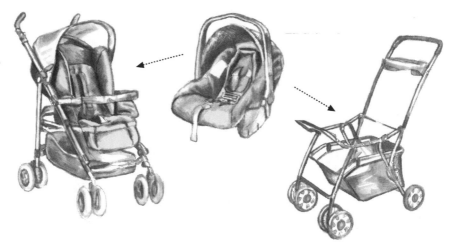

Travel Systems and Car Seat Carriers provide two ways to take your baby from the car into the stroller without removing her from the car seat. **Travel Systems** are basic strollers with special adapters that let you snap an infant car seat on top of the stroller seat, making it safe for newborns. Some travel systems are sold with their own car seats, and others support a variety of brands. In general, they tend to be bulky. **Car Seat Carriers** consist of a simple stroller frame and wheels, and you just snap your car seat into and out of the frame at will. They fold up to the size of a metal folding chair, weigh about 10 pounds, and are relatively cheap.

Lightweight Strollers weigh anywhere from 9 to 18 pounds and are great for urban dwellers. The best ones are surprisingly sturdy (and surprisingly expensive), and offer spring-into-action open-and-fold technology. Some newer models come with seats that fold all the way back so that newborns can use them, and others feature attachment bars for car seat hook-ups. The small wheels are a drawback on rough terrain, and the undersized storage basket forces many parents to hang bags from the handles, which can unbalance the unit. (Adding counterweights to the front wheels solves this problem.)

Lightweight strollers can tip.

Umbrella Strollers are the Chevy Vegas of the stroller world. They are cheap, ultra-light, flimsy, and ultimately disposable. Features include a piece of fabric over a frame. If you are traveling and need something really light to use in airports, these are recommended. Otherwise, steer clear (when closing they tend to collapse on your fingers).

Joggers are the SUVs of the stroller world. These three-wheeled beasts have a very high wheel base, which is optimal in the event of a stroller-on-stroller collision. They are perfect for extreme and wilderness strolling, but their size and weight make them impractical for everyday use. They shouldn't be used until babies can support their heads. And no matter how gung ho you are about running, never buy a jogger until well after the baby is born. Then see how much you want to run. More often than not, joggers become hampers as soon as the baby arrives.

Stealth Strollers are pieces of equipment that have strollers hidden inside them. So far they've come up with backpack strollers, where the backpack frame becomes the stroller body, and car seat strollers, where the entire stroller is hidden inside the base of the car seat. Look for the diaper stroller in the fall of 2008.

Some Useful Accessories
(sold separately):
- Plastic Rain Hood
- Boot—protects baby's feet in cold weather
- U/V Canopy—for sun protection
- Cup Holder—for your single malt
- Activity Tray with Snack Holder
- Clamp-on Mesh Bag—for extra storage

The Infant Ensemble

You are looking at the most important piece of clothing your baby will own during the first year of her life. It's the perfect blend of comfort and functionality, works as sleepwear and leisurewear, and complements your baby's body shape and active lifestyle. Whether lounging around the house or cruising around in the stroller, the feetsie pajama is the way to go. (Some people call them sleepers.)

And best of all, there are no neck holes. Babies hate putting their heads through neck holes, perhaps thinking that you're trying to stuff them back into the womb. Feetsie pajamas open from the neck all the way to the ankle (via a zipper or snaps), so you just lay them on top of it, and guide their limbs through the appropriate holes.

And the icing on the cake: when your baby outgrows them, just cut off the feet and you've got regular pajamas. Slap some socks on her and you are good to go.

Now your partner may try to throw the concept of aesthetics into the mix, choosing, against all logic, to bedeck the baby in jumpers and rompers and tights and leggings, things from Italy with tiny neck holes and inaccessible crotches. Although it's useless to fight her on this, you can always change the baby back into her pj's whenever you're on duty.

Dads don't dress their babies like this.

DRESSING FOR HOT AND COLD

Your baby doesn't need any more clothing than you do, and she'll usually tell you, by fussing, if she's too hot or cold. If you want a gauge, check the back of her neck. If it feels either too cold or hot and sweaty, adjust clothing accordingly. In cold weather, it's best to dress your baby in layers that you can take off and put on as the temperature shifts. And if she needs mittens, stick a pair of baby socks on her hands.

In the sleep sack your baby looks like she's about to pupate.

Winter Sleeping

When it gets really cold, you may need a layer over your baby's feetsie pajamas at bedtime, but blankets have been deemed unsafe for young babies. That's where the sleep sack comes in. A sleeveless, collarless wearable blanket, the sleep sack makes your baby look like a giant larva, but it keeps her from kicking off her covers, a common baby trick.

The Sun

Treat your baby like a vampire for the first six months, keeping her out of direct sunlight as much as possible. When you do go out with her, try to cover her up with loose, long-sleeve clothing.

Once she hits six months, you can venture out into the sun for limited periods, but be sure to slather baby sunscreen on all unclothed areas. Also get her a pair of sunglasses to protect her eyes, but don't be surprised if they wind up on the ground more than on her face. A lightweight flap hat (see above) will also keep the glare out of her eyes, and protect her head and neck in the process.

Summer Sleeping

What do you do when it's too hot for feetsie pajamas? Try this little number here. It's called a onesie, and it's a no-brainer. Loose neck, crotch snaps—what's not to like? Unsnapped, it looks like your baby's wearing tails.

And if the neck hole is too small, you can stretch it around a two-liter plastic soda bottle for a couple of hours to loosen it up.

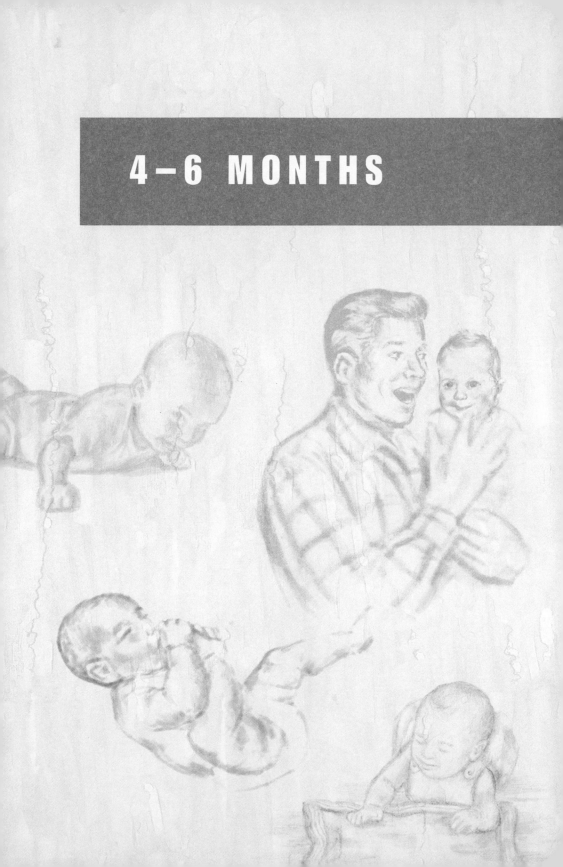

4–6 MONTHS

You've probably begun to realize that most of the time spent with babies this age is not so much quality time as it is *quantity time*— endless hours of routine bodily maintenance, punctuated by knee-bouncing, song-singing, and the occasional staring contest. You look at your watch thinking that two hours have gone by, and a mere fifteen minutes has ticked off.

After a while, the isolation and lack of mental stimulation can start to drive you insane. You may find yourself eagerly picking up the phone for telemarketers, thankful for any adult interaction; staring transfixed at a baby video for half an hour after your baby's fallen asleep next to you; and, without realizing it, ending all of your conversations with a high-pitched "bye-bye." Is your brain starting to curdle? And what can you do about it?

Some steps you can take to regain some semblance of mental stability:

- **Create a Sanctuary.** Claim one room in the house for your own and keep it 100% baby-free. (If you live in a small apartment, claim a walk-in closet.) Make the room a tribute to your former life.

Before you forget everything, archive your memories on a wall calendar.

Display your old concert posters, stolen street signs, bongo drums, your giant foam #1 finger, the hood ornament from your first set of wheels, and the shrunken head your uncle brought back from Singapore. Whenever the baby naps, retreat to the sanctuary for some peace of mind.

- **Get Some Ink on Your Fingers.** Life with a baby is life in a vacuum. To keep yourself connected to the world, read the paper whenever you get the chance. This way, the next time you enter into an adult conversation, you'll have something to talk about besides the latest swaddling techniques.

- **Maintain Your Fighting Weight.** Some dads experience a sympathetic pregnancy after the baby comes, a result of eating odd things at odd hours and getting almost no exercise. But it's important to stay within range of your pre-baby weight, not only because you'll feel better, but also because once the baby starts to crawl, you'll have to leap up and pounce at a moment's notice. Lose half a step and your camcorder may be toast.

- **Take Off.** Inside time is much slower than outside time. So when you're with the baby, and the second hand on your watch starts freezing over, pack him up and go somewhere. Anywhere. Take a trip to the auto parts store. Let him feel some tire tread and look at all the shiny hubcaps.

- **Find Other Dads.** If you want to feel better about your brand-new life, don't hang out with single guys. Even though you keep telling yourself their lives are empty and devoid of higher purpose, it's hard not to get jealous of their freedom. But spend some time with other new dads, and you end up feeling much better about yourself. Drudgery loves company.

- **Take Notes.** Chances are that you were given one of those baby scrapbooks, and it hasn't been filled out for at least a month. Instead, try putting up a big monthly wall calendar somewhere in your house (the kitchen is optimal). Unlike a scrapbook, you'll always be able to find it and fill it out while holding the baby. Whenever something interesting happens, just write it down. You can also tape photos onto the pages. At the end of each month, rip off the page and store it somewhere safe for future reference.

Looking at the calendar serves the dual purpose of reminding you that, a) no, time hasn't been standing still, and b) embedded within the drudgery are some truly amazing and memorable moments. Savor these moments, for you will never pass this way again, at least with this child.

Resuming a SEX Life?

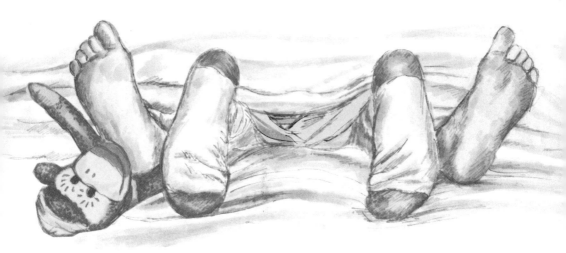

Before you start panicking about your sex life (or lack thereof) after the baby arrives, consider the following: in a recent study published in the *Journal of Family Practice,* at least 50% of the couples polled had resumed sex at around two months, and more than 90% of couples had hooked up by the four-month mark. So you can pretty well assume that you'll be back in business by day 120 (with heartfelt condolences going out to the other 10%).

Although you may feel that four months is an eternity, consider the fact that it will take you at least that long to get the memory of the birth out of your head. There's no arguing that the birth of your baby is a miraculous event, but the experience of seeing that giant slimy head emerging from your partner's uterus is a bit scary, as anyone who's seen the movie *Alien* can attest.

Once you're ready, willing, and able, you've got to wait until your partner feels the same way. Until then, just bide your time. And it might be a good idea to get yourself a high-speed internet connection.

Why Your Partner May Be Giving You the Cold Shoulder

- Her hormones are suppressing her sex drive, making sure she cares for this baby instead of creating a new one.

- Her body's just pulled off a Houdini-like feat, and is healing.

- She's most likely been sucked, kneaded, pawed, and screamed at all day, and she may not want to be sucked, kneaded, pawed, or screamed at by anyone else for a while.

- She doesn't fit into her clothes anymore, which can lead to fears that you don't find her attractive. Do everything you can to convince her otherwise.

Regreasing the Wheels

The prepared dad knows that foreplay doesn't begin in the bedroom, and it doesn't begin right before sex.

- As soon as possible, set aside one night a week where you and your partner can be baby-free, even for just an hour or two. Go bowling, play pool, see a movie. Anything that brings even a tiny bit of balance back into your lives is good.

- Humor is a great aphrodisiac. Surprise her by writing notes on the baby's diaper with a Sharpie, making sure that she'll be the next one to change him, and not your mother-in-law.

- Pretend that intimacy is more important to you than sex. This may be hard to pull off, considering you're going against millions of years of male heredity. But pressuring your partner will do you no good. So at this point, let a cuddle be an end rather than a means.

- Drop subtle hints. You can say things like, "I read somewhere that sex has been shown to reduce stress and ease back and neck pain. Not only that, but it also can help your skin retain elasticity and retard the aging process. Isn't that interesting?" By the way, all of this is true.

- If you are nearing the breaking point, you may want to ask her if she's willing to do anything at all to help you overcome your frustration. After all, not all of her body parts are sore. In exchange, you can promise to take the baby out for an entire day so she can have time to herself. Get used to this type of bartering, as it's an essential part of the parental dynamic.

The Big Night

When will she be ready to unfreeze your membership card? It's hard to tell. Never assume that today's the day, but always be prepared just in case.

- Be shaved and showered as often as possible.

- Have a designated shoebox where you store the lubricants (absolutely essential for post-partum sex), condoms (she can get pregnant again sooner than you think), and mood enhancers such as alcohol, candles, massage oils, favorite music, etc.

- Never, ever wake your partner for sex. It's like taking food away from a wild animal.

- Don't try to engage in the same room with the baby. Sixty percent of couples eventually do, but the first time back is tense enough without a grunting, shifting baby five feet away from you.

   - No matter where you choose to connect, sweep the area for baby toys first, as you don't want to roll over mid-session and activate Barney's "I Love You" song.

   - Time your escapade to coincide with your baby's deepest sleep state, which on average starts between fifteen and twenty minutes after you put him down. But be aware that babies seem to have a sixth sense when it comes to their parents' sexual activity, choosing the most inopportune moments to start crying. Perhaps their instincts are telling them to eliminate potential competition.

Protecting Your BACK

Being a guy, much of the heavy lifting is likely to fall on your shoulders (literally). Be prepared to carry the baby for long stretches of time, haul around all of his gear, bend and twist to get him in and out of the car seat, hoist the stroller out of the trunk, and occasionally pick up your partner just to prove to her that she hasn't gotten any heavier since the pregnancy.

Is it any wonder that in a given year at least 50% of all men experience some sort of back pain?

Joining a gym at this point would most likely be an act of blind optimism, and could be frowned upon by your overwhelmed, under-exercised partner. This means that you've got to find a way to shore up your back while on the baby clock. Here are some exercises to get you started. (For video clips of proper technique, go to www.beprepared.net.)

Sticker Twist Crunches

Muscles Used: Abs, Obliques

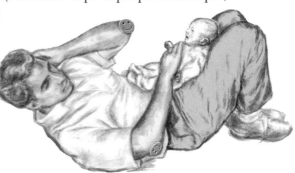

1. Affix a big happy face sticker (anything with a pattern will do) on your left elbow.

2. Lie on your back with your knees bent and your feet on the floor.

3. Place the baby against your thighs and hold him steady with your right hand, while placing your left hand slightly behind your head, fingers touching your ear.

4. As you breathe out, slowly bring your left elbow toward the baby until your shoulder comes off the floor. Try to bring the sticker about twelve inches away from the baby's face.

5. Hold for three seconds while squeezing your abs, and then breathe in as you lower your back down to the floor.

6. Repeat, and then switch elbows.

Start out with two sets of ten reps each.

Car Seat Bends

Muscles Used: Obliques

1. Stand with your feet about shoulder-width apart and your back straight.

2. Hold the car seat or carrier (with the baby strapped in) in your left hand. Place your right hand on your waist.

3. Slowly bend to the left as far as you can go, and then slowly return to starting position.

Start out with two sets of ten reps on each arm.

In this exercise, you are using the baby as a dumbbell.

Carrier Wall Slides

Muscles Used: Back, Hips, Quadriceps

1. With your baby in the front carrier, stand with your back against a wall and your feet shoulder-width apart.

2. Slide down the wall until your knees are bent at a 45- to 60-degree angle. Keep your abdominals tight.

3. Count to five and slide back up.

Start with two sets of five to ten reps each and slowly increase the reps and duration of each rep. This exercise gets much more difficult as the baby grows.

Circuit Training
Your BABY

Hanging out with the baby and looking for a good way to kill half an hour? Try setting up all of his apparatus in the living room and have him do a little circuit training. The baby will get his first taste of a gym workout, and you can be his personal trainer, shuffling him from station to station and shouting out "All you! All you!" as you put him through his paces.

In the adult world, circuit training is a series of exercises, normally done on machines, designed to give you a quick and effective full-body workout. The baby circuit works the same way. When your baby has completed the circuit, he'll have developed his muscles, coordination, and balance. Keep up the routine and you'll have the buffest baby in the sandbox.

As you're setting up the stations, keep in mind that you don't want to repeat similar exercises back-to-back. You want to give those mini-muscles some time to rest between sets. Spend about five minutes at each station, and take a short break in between. And if your small fry starts to get restless before you've completed the circuit, preempt the workout and go straight to the cool down. Those buns of steel will have to wait until next time.

1st
STOP

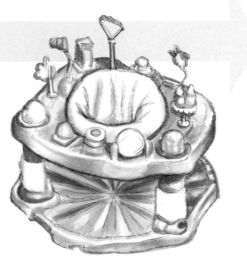

The Exersaucer is a two-tiered contraption with a round base and a cloth seat. Babies are positioned upright, which helps develop core muscles (abs and back).

2nd STOP

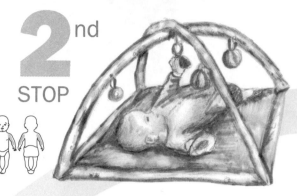

The Gymini is a popular toy that combines a playmat with a crossbar. There are holes at various points in the crossbar, allowing you to hang toys just out of your baby's reach. As he swings his arms at the toys, he's developing the biceps and triceps and gross motor skills.

3rd STOP

The Jumper consists of a bucket seat and some bungee cords, and you hang it in a doorway. Babies tend to love the jumper and you may be tempted to leave them in there for as long as they are enjoying themselves. But overuse of the jumper can be a bit hard on a baby's joints. This works the baby's gluteals, quads, and calf muscles.

4th STOP

Facedown on the Play Mat
is one of babies' least favorite activities, but most important.
When he's on his stomach, he has to struggle to keep his head and neck up to look around. This develops the neck and back muscles, which are important in crawling.

7th

STOP

The Swing is the perfect relaxing cool down, and often the best way to get your baby to take a well-deserved nap. Besides, he'll be outgrowing the swing soon, so take advantage while you can.

6th

STOP

The Boppy Pillow helps to support the baby as he learns to sit. Place him seated in this pillow with some favorite toys in front of him. Helps develop back and abdominal muscles.

5th

STOP

The Kicking Gym has hanging lights and noise toys. When your baby successfully kicks the toys, he gets a little show. Good for lower-body strength, gross motor skills, and depth perception.

Tethering EVERYTHING
to the Baby

Throwing things must be intensely satisfying for babies— watching the object disappear, hearing the thud/splat, catching Dad's animated reaction, and then seeing it reappear on the horizon.

Until you find a way to batten down everything in the baby's immediate vicinity, you'll have to deal with his tendency to throw or drop everything he touches. Bottles and pacifiers covered in dirt, toys abandoned in mall parking lots, and bowls of cereal splattered all over the kitchen floor. You'll also have a sore back from playing the "I throw it, you pick it up" game.

The good news is there are many different fastening options available (see below), and pretty much every object can be secured either to the baby or whatever contraption he happens to be inhabiting at the moment.

A word of caution: If you are thinking about making your own cords, keep in mind that anything over five inches long is considered a strangulation hazard.

suction cup bowls

suction cup toys

pacifier cords

bottle holders

GERMS AND THE FIVE-SECOND RULE

The Five-Second Rule states that if the baby drops something on the floor and you pick it up within five seconds, the object is not yet officially "dirty." However, once you have passed the five-second mark, washing becomes necessary.

Although never clinically proven, the Five-Second Rule has been accepted as gospel by fathers all over the world. In general, moms tend to be more vigilant when it comes to cleanliness, but there's reason to believe that a more relaxed approach may not be such a bad thing (within reason, of course). Here are some arguments for leniency:

The Third Child. It's common knowledge that parents get lazier and lazier with each child, and by the third, very little sterilization is going on. As one dad put it, "When our first dropped the pacifier, I'd run it under soap and water before giving it back to him. With our second, I'd wipe it off on my shirt. With the third, I just kick it back to him." Yet these third children seem to turn out just as healthy and robust as their more sanitized siblings.

Germs Aren't Everywhere. An informal study done at the University of Illinois tested dozens of locations around campus—the cafeteria, the library, in front of vending machines—and found the numbers of bacteria on the floor were remarkably low in all locations. To test the Five-Second Rule, they had to spread *E. coli* bacteria on floor tiles and drop food directly on them. And, yes, the food was contaminated within five seconds. So the lesson here is this: If your baby drops something into a pile of poop, don't give it back to him, no matter how quickly you pick it up.

How Germs Spread. Most babies get their germs the old-fashioned way—from other babies. Day care centers, playgrounds, those rooms full of rubber balls—they are all basically giant petri dishes where babies swap microbes. You can try to control where he plays and who he plays with, but usually by the time a parent knows their kid is sick, yours has already been exposed.

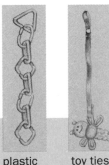

plastic baby links   toy ties

Your Time. If you were to sterilize something every time your baby dropped it, you'd have no time to actually interact with him.

TEMPERATURE
Taking Tactics

There's no fun and easy way to take your baby's temperature. You can try:

- the ear thermometer, which can be wildly inaccurate, especially for very young babies,

- the armpit method, which is a bit more reliable, but the readings can be consistently low,

- the hand-on-the-forehead technique, which will give you a general idea, or

- the rectal thermometer, by far the most accurate but humiliating method. Hopefully the baby will block this from memory.

If you're going to take the rectal route, be sure to purchase a flexible digital rectal thermometer, as opposed to the old-fashioned glass thermometer, which could possibly break. Sterilize it with alcohol, rinse it with warm water, dry it off, and then slather some baby-safe lubricant onto the tip.

How do you keep the baby still while taking his temperature? Obviously this process is easier with your partner's help. But in case you are flying solo, here is a dad-proven technique for holding your baffled, uncomfortable baby steady during the occupation:

1. Place two pillows on top of one another on the floor, and lay a towel over the pillows.

2. Take off the baby's diaper and lay him facedown so that his stomach is on top of the pillows. Spread his cheeks and insert the thermometer about an inch deep.

3. Hold the thermometer in place by laying your hand flush against your baby's buttocks with the thermometer in between the index and middle fingers. This way if the baby bucks, your hand and the thermometer will move with him.

4. Use the other hand to animate a stuffed animal, making it dance around, sing, talk to the baby, whatever it takes.

5. Most digital thermometers beep when the temperature has been successfully ascertained. Check the results, apologize profusely to the baby, and, if necessary, take appropriate action.

Treating a Fever

A fever by itself isn't the best gauge of a baby's health. Behavior changes—listlessness, crankiness, non-stop crying—are even better indicators of a sick baby and should be dealt with by calling the pediatrician.

Regarding a fever, here are some general guidelines:

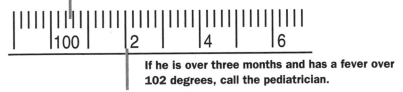

If he is younger than three months old and has a temperature of 100.5 degrees or above, call the pediatrician.

If he is over three months and has a fever over 102 degrees, call the pediatrician.

Some common fever-reducing tactics include anti-fever medication, lukewarm baths, cool compresses, and plenty of fluids.

Getting Medicine into a BABY

If you want to earn your stripes as a dad, you've got to become a first-class medicine giver. This will involve smarts, stamina, and, at times, outright treachery, as the baby will almost surely put up resistance.

Some ways to get the medicine down:

Turn It into a Game. "See— medicine is fun!" Take turns "feeding" the meds to your partner, yourself, a stuffed animal, and then baby.

Mask the Taste. Some medicines can be mixed with food or frozen (check with the pharmacist). Stir it into a bowl of applesauce or mix it with a small amount of milk in the baby's bottle. Freeze it (dulling its taste), and pour chocolate syrup on top of it. If you're using a syringe or dropper, try rolling it around in a bowl of sugar.

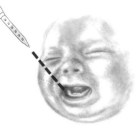

Bypass the Buds. Using a dropper or syringe, aim for the area between the cheek and lower gum, toward the back (see left). If you are lucky, the medicine may just slide right down his throat without incident.

Resort to Deceit. If you are desperate, you can try the Trojan horse method—a modified pacifier that, once inside baby's mouth, squirts medicine. But be warned: he may get very upset by this betrayal, as the pacifier was one of the few reliable things in

104

his life. You can also feed the baby ice cream, and after five or six bites, when his mouth's open wide, quickly shoot in a stream of medicine followed by a quick spoonful of ice cream. He may not know what hit him.

Change Flavors, Strengths, or Forms. Medicines come in a multitude of flavors, so if one doesn't work, try another. Some prescriptions come in different strengths. Always opt for the stronger dosage, because that means you'll have to give the baby less of it. Or you may be able to bypass the mouth entirely if suppositories are available.

MEDICINE AND THE ORNERY BABY

Some babies just don't know what's good for them. Since there's no choice but to get the medicine down, you may have to resort to the steer rustler technique:

1. Prop a pillow up against one arm of the couch, and spread a towel over the couch arm for stain control.

2. Wrap your baby in a blanket, pinning his hands against his sides.

3. Lay him up against the pillow. Make sure that he's not lying flat (so he won't choke).

4. Sit on the edge of the couch, lean over him, and gently but firmly hold his chin steady with one hand while squirting a small amount of medicine into his cheek pocket (see previous page) with the other.

5. Gently blow into the baby's face. This triggers the swallow reflex.

6. Repeat 4 and 5 until all of the medicine is gone.

7. Thank the baby and tell him to see the receptionist on the way out.

Soothing the TEETHER

Michelangelo's
The Teethers

If your baby starts drooling uncontrollably, becomes irritated for no apparent reason, wakes up every hour, and tries to gum everything in sight, congratulations are in order! He's entering the ranks of the toothed.

But celebrating this new milestone is probably the last thing on your mind. "Why me?" is probably the first. Just when you start breathing a little sigh of relief—the baby is sleeping for longer stretches, you and your partner are back on speaking terms—the onset of teething is an abrupt reminder that serenity is a fragile and fleeting concept.

On average, baby's first tooth arrives between six and seven months, but symptoms can appear months before the tooth actually rears its little pointy head (you can sometimes feel a bump just under the gum). Along with the symptoms listed above, red cheeks, a chin rash, diarrhea, a low-grade fever, inflamed or bleeding gums, and a refusal to feed have also been associated with teething.

But by far the most obvious sign is the absurd volume of drool streaming down his chin at all times, making him look like one of those tacky cherub fountains you find in some people's backyards.

He may soak through five or six outfits a day.

As pediatricians are quick to point out, these symptoms can be indicative of other conditions as well, so if they persist, or if you have any concerns, call your doctor.

Your Teething Toolbox

When you were teething, your parents might have rubbed whisky on your gums, a proven old country remedy that doctors today will not prescribe. Perhaps they're afraid you'll give your baby crib spins, or perhaps they fear you'll self-medicate and pass out on his changing table. The truth is that alcohol is a toxin, and too much could harm the baby.

Since Jack Daniels is out of the picture, here are some alternate offerings:

Your knuckles and fingers Your knuckles seem to be the perfect size and firmness for chewing, and applying gentle pressure on the afflicted area with your finger can also provide relief.

Teething toys Many teething toys have bumps and nodules for the baby to gnaw on, but young teethers may not have the dexterity to hold them in place. You can also use a little baby toothbrush that you place over the end of your finger. The bristles relieve the teething itch.

Random frozen objects There are many things that, when placed in the freezer, become teething toys. Spoons, bananas, bagels, carrots, pacifiers, and washcloths can be frozen and applied to the gum. But once the tooth breaks through, be careful about the baby biting off chunks of the frozen foods (the same applies to store-bought teething biscuits).

Frozen bagels can be tethered to the baby, stroller, or high chair.

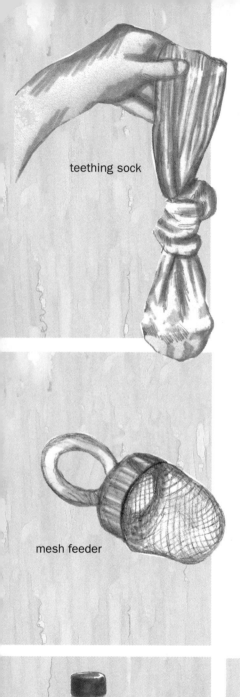

teething sock

mesh feeder

You can create an effective homemade teether by placing crushed ice or frozen apple slices inside a clean sock. Once the sock is knotted, the baby can hold it and chew on the contents (and he can get the flavor from the apples). You can buy a mesh fruit feeder to approximate this device.

Teething gels These over-the-counter topical anesthetics numb the gum tissue, and can provide immediate relief. Though fast-acting, the effect doesn't last very long, and you can only apply the gel three or four times a day.

Acetaminophen This is perhaps the most effective way to deal with nighttime teething issues. The active ingredient in Infant Tylenol, acetaminophen, or, as it's known on the streets, Liquid Nap, works for up to four hours, giving you at least a shot at four hours of sleep. Make sure to consult your pediatrician before giving the baby any medicine. (For help getting medicine into your baby, see pg. 104.)

teething gel

baby toothbrush

Tooth Maintenance

You wouldn't wash your car on the way to the junkyard. So why would you take care of a baby tooth if it's just going to fall out anyway? Well, here are three important reasons why tooth maintenance needs to be an important part of your routine:

- Baby teeth are placeholders for adult teeth, and losing them early could distort the shape of your baby's mouth.

- Baby teeth don't fall out for another five years, so if you want your baby to enjoy a nice juicy steak, you'd better take care of those teeth now.

- Unless he plans on going into hip hop, it would be a bit startling for your baby's only tooth to have a big gold cap on it.

To keep his tooth clean, you can wipe it off daily with a washcloth, gauze pad, or baby toothbrush. Toothpaste is not necessary at this point. Also, don't let him sleep for long periods with a bottle or breast in his mouth because the sugar from the milk can cause decay. Make sure he gets enough fluoride, either by drinking tap water or taking fluoride supplements. And when he hits the two-year mark, you can take him to the pediatric dentist.

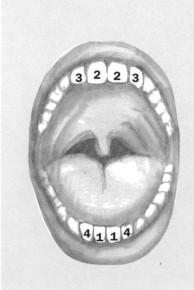

Order of Tooth Development

1s erupt between 6 and 10 months

2s erupt between 7 and 11 months

3s erupt between 8 and 12 months

4s erupt between 9 and 13 months

This is just an average. Some babies don't get a tooth until after their first birthday, and a few even come out of the womb flashing a pearly white. (The tooth is removed so it won't fall out and become a choking hazard.)

Be Prepared
for OUTINGS

Getting out of the house with the baby is like moving the Pope. There is a ridiculous amount of paraphernalia that you have to lug around. And for some reason the size of the baby is inversely proportional to the weight of the load.

One of the biggest advantages that dads have over moms is our ability to get out of the house quickly. That is because dads embrace one of the cardinal laws of parenthood:

Once you've managed to get out of the house with the baby, don't go back in no matter what.

If you've forgotten something, either buy a new one or take your chances without it. But if you make it a policy to keep going back for stuff, eventually you'll become paralyzed with indecision and you'll never leave.

Many dads get a case of the cold sweats when faced with their first solo field trip with the small fry. After all, you haven't even mastered in-home care, where there's plenty of food, shelter, equipment, and immediate access to emergency services. So what makes you think you can survive in the field?

In a word, preparation!

The G.I. Tool Bag

YOUR GEAR BAG

Most likely your partner has something called a diaper bag, and chances are it looks like a big purse. Do you really want to lug this around with you? Instead, you can just use a gym bag or an old backpack and stuff all of your baby items in that. So what if there isn't a special pocket for wipes. Do you need to be that organized? If you have to buy something, then go down to an army-navy store and get a G.I. Tool Bag. They're pretty cheap, lightweight, and made out of heavy-duty canvas. And they have enough room and pockets for all of your supplies. How many other diaper bags have been tested on the battlefield?

There are eight basic items that belong in your gear bag:

1. **Diapers**—at least two more than you think you'll need.

2. **Wipes**—for everything from fluid containment to toy sterilization.

3. **Plastic Bags**—to deposit used diapers, wipes, and soiled clothes in.

4. **Changing Pad**—to put down under the baby during changes.

5. **Bottles**—Breast milk can be stored in bottles along with cold packs in a small bottle bag. Powdered formula can be put in a zipper bag and poured into bottles full of water.

6. **Burp Cloth**—so you won't walk around smelling like spit-up.

7. **Clothes**—for you and baby—a complete outfit for him and an extra shirt for you just in case.

8. **Toys**—Age-appropriate toys provide stimulation or distraction to head off a crying jag.

Don't worry about memorizing this list. In the sentence below, the first letter of each word is also the first letter of one of the items on your list. Memorize the sentence and you'll never be left holding the bag.

> **" TEENAGERS WITH BABIES DON'T PRACTICE CAREFUL BIRTH CONTROL. "**

Now, if you feel that this particular sentence will have trouble sticking to your brain, try one of these alternatives:

DAD'S BACK PROBLEMS CAUSED BY CARRYING WEIGHTY TODDLER.

BABIES CAN'T BE DRY-CLEANED, PUT THROUGH WASH.

Supplementary Items

Because you ought to be prepared for everything, you may want to take along the following additional materials:

Multi-Tool—Pocket tools like the Leatherman are useful for everything from opening formula to stroller repairs.

Duct Tape—Good for stroller and carrier repair, emergency diaper fastening, etc.

Extra Pacifiers—Even if you have one tethered to his shirt, it's always good to have an extra three or four.

Spit-up Resistant Watch—Diving watches are optimal. If they can survive 300 feet below sea level, your baby's discharge should be no problem.

Keychain Toy—Even though it looks goofy, clip a toy or small stuffed animal to your keychain. For situations where you need immediate distraction, it's the ace in your deck.

Camera—If your cell phone doesn't come equipped with one, take a camera along. You never know when that e-mail-worthy shot just happens to come along.

Be sure to tuck an extra car key in your wallet for emergency situations. More than one sleep-deprived dad has locked his keys in the car with the baby still in the backseat.

You may think this will never happen to you, and it probably won't, but stick the key in your wallet anyway. The difficulty of pacifying a six-month-old through a car window is only matched by the humiliation of explaining to the 911 operator the nature of your emergency.

Up until now, you could take your baby just about anywhere and he'd probably have a similar stone-faced reaction. But by 4–6 months, your baby's burgeoning personality is starting to emerge, and he will definitely prefer some activities over others.

- **Supermarkets** The dazzling array of colors, textures, and sounds will really excite the baby. Have him feel different products—a crinkling bag of chips versus a cold frozen turkey. And definitely try to catch the spraying of the produce.

- **Pet Stores** The chirping birds, gurgling fish tanks, hamsters, and lizards can keep the baby transfixed for long periods of time. If you feel guilty about loitering, buy a squeaky dog toy for him to play with.

- **Escalators** Riding up and down escalators helps with his growing sense of depth perception and object tracking, and he'll be sure to get smiles and waves from everyone coming the other way. (But *NEVER* use the stroller on an escalator.)

- **Art Museums** In general, most babies enjoy realism, especially portraits of people and animals where the faces are clearly discernible. Sculpture also engages them, as do paintings with large clean shapes.

- **Happy Hour** caters to single people to whom the baby is a novelty, so he'll have plenty of built-in entertainment. But the place has got to be smoke-free, and you need to arrive before people are drunk, and leave before the baby gets cranky. Perch your baby on an open pool table to play with all of the colorful balls, or flip the jukebox CD racks as he watches.

Driving and CRYING

When you've got a baby in the car, you drive with a sense of purpose normally associated with ambulance drivers and New York City cabbies. You know that at any moment the niblet could start screaming. And if you have ever been trapped alone in a traffic jam with a screaming baby in the backseat, then you know what desperation feels like.

There are certain times where you have to stop the car to remedy the situation. If he's wet, you have to change him. If he's hungry, you have to give him a bottle (but if he's on solids, you can clip a snack cup to the car seat). If he's bothered by the glare, you can attach a sun visor to the window. But for everything else, you can alleviate backseat blubbering by employing the following tactics:

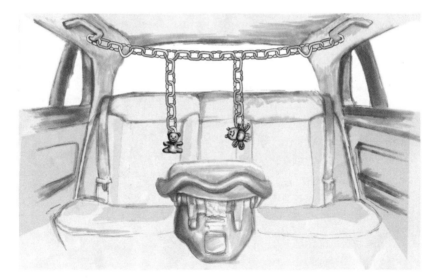

- String up plastic baby linking chains across the backseat, attached to the handles above the rear windows. Hang soft toys from the links. Every time you pull over you can take off old toys and put new ones on. Just make sure the chain doesn't obstruct your view, and that the toys are hung at a perfect height for a baby to reach out and bat them around.

Tape photos onto a towel to keep your baby occupied in transit.

- Keep a box full of toys next to you in the front seat and hand them back to the baby one-by-one. Remember, you can't pick things up when he drops them, so it's recommended that you load up at the beginning of each trip. Multiple pacifiers are good to have on hand as well.

- Duct-tape some family pictures and black-and-white patterns to a towel (or directly to the upholstery if it's a rental) and drape it over the backseat with tape at the top so it won't fall down. Make sure the pictures are secure as you don't want baby chewing on them. You can also buy something called a car seat gallery that has little clear pockets for pictures.

- If you think the baby is overtired, turn the radio dial to white noise or open the windows to get a whooshing sound. If you are stuck in bumper-to-bumper traffic, you can press and release the brake to create a rocking motion.

- Play the radio loudly on scan until you find a song that quiets the baby.

THE MIRROR PUPPET SING-ALONG

This little-known technique usually works when all else fails.

You will need three things:

- A soft hand puppet that you can wear without impairing your driving ability.

- A mirror that clips onto the backseat and tilts so that the baby can see you and you can see him through your rearview mirror. This is a good item to have for any car trip, because it gives you a view of the baby. (There's one called *The Car Seat Companion* that's available online.)

- A CD or tape of baby songs.

Directions:

Place the puppet on your hand and make sure the baby can see it in his mirror. Get his attention by talking in a loud, obnoxious puppet voice. Turn on the CD player and sing along, manipulating the puppet's mouth as you go. The baby will think he's watching TV. But always remember to keep your eyes on the road.

The people in cars on either side of you probably won't be able to see the baby and may think you insane. But that's the price you pay for a quiet baby.

Using the Baby
as a PROP

Men with babies come across as more honest, sensitive, and responsible than their baby-less counterparts. Whereas without the baby women might see you as a predator and men as competition, with the baby you are a big, harmless lug to all.

As much as you'd like to rail against this prejudice, don't. Instead, why not take advantage of your sudden sainthood? Whenever you need to negotiate with someone, bring the baby along for leverage.

When preparing the baby for the sting, you should try to make sure that he's bathed, changed, and awake. It might also be a good idea to have your partner dress him. Remember: you're going for maximum cuteness here.

Some suggestions:

Returning an Item without a Receipt
For best results, place the baby in the car seat right up on the customer service counter. If you get any resistance, you can say that the baby may in fact have eaten the receipt, and you'll be glad to take off his diaper and look for it.

Jury Duty
Take your baby on a field trip and teach him the loopholes of the legal system at the same time. With a squirming baby in your lap, there's no doubt you'll be sent home early.

Getting Prime Seats
When you take the baby to a sporting event, tip the usher and tell him that this is the baby's first game and you'd love him to be able to see the action up close.

Getting "Bumped Up" in Long Lines
This one can go both ways. People may invite you to cut ahead of them if they see you with a baby, or they may just sneer and pretend they don't notice you. But if there's a full diaper involved, the odds are in your favor.

Picking Up the Girls
If you are a single dad, just walk around the mall and wait for the feeding frenzy. If you are married, why not lend the baby out to a single friend? Of course you should be there as back-up, but don't walk alongside him. People might assume that he's spoken for.

Taking a Sick Day
Now that you have the baby, you have so many more excuses to play hooky from work. You're sick, the baby's sick, the babysitter never showed up, and so on. Before calling the boss, download the crying baby clip from www.beprepared.net and play it in the background. With it, your boss won't have the nerve to question you.

Breastfeeding in PUBLIC

The term "breastfeeding in public" almost implies an audience. But, depending upon the venue, it can be done discreetly. Department stores have dressing rooms, movie theaters are dark, bookstores have a philosophy section. But other places, particularly restaurants, offer few viable options, meaning your partner can either feed at the table or trundle over to the rustic ambience of the restroom. By the way, a mother's right to nurse anywhere she pleases is protected by law.

If you are at all nervous about other men ogling your partner's breasts in public, don't be. The vast majority of men are not turned on by nursing moms. If anything, it makes them uncomfortable. And having a conversation with someone who's feeding is almost impossible. No one knows where to focus their eyes. Which is why, if you are ever dining with friends and your partner starts nursing, it's your job to take over the conversation. Talk about sports, movies, the weather, anything. Well, not anything. You should probably avoid mentioning the succulent chicken breast or your trip to Naples. And for God's sake don't order the melon.

To ensure your partner's privacy, you can drape your jacket over her shoulder while she feeds, shielding her breast and the baby from view. Make sure the jacket isn't too close to the baby's face or so heavy that he becomes overheated.

STARTING
Solid
Foods

New fatherhood is full of memorable moments, but perhaps none will surpass watching your baby's face as he takes his first spoonful of solid food. You can almost guarantee that no matter how bland the offering may be, your baby will react as if you have just given him a double shot of Jagermeister. This moment is too precious to squint at through a video monitor. So if you decide to tape it (and you should), set the camera on a tripod or stack of books so that your eyes are free to witness the quivering, horrified expression firsthand.

Ironically, this is pretty much the same expression you'll exhibit upon opening up the first solid-food diaper. Now that the baby is starting to eat like one of us, he'll be evacuating like one of us as well. Suddenly you'll realize how good you had it those first few months.

Before introducing solids, read the following:

- Wait until your baby is at least four months old. Very young babies have a tongue-thrust reflex that prevents them from choking, but also makes it almost impossible to get solid food to the back of the throat. Also, young babies' intestines aren't able to properly hold in nutrients and filter out harmful substances.

- If your baby is able to sit up in a high chair, lunges for your French fries, or pretends to chew when he sees you chewing, he's probably ready to start on solid foods.

- To make sure he doesn't have food allergies, introduce one food for three consecutive days before moving on to the next one. If your baby has a reaction, you'll know which food is the culprit.

Useful tips for successful solid-food delivery:

A bath mat on the high chair will prevent sliding.

No-Slip the Seat. If your baby is slipping around in the high chair, cut a square piece of a bath mat and suction it onto the seat.

Contain the Mess. If you don't have a dog, you'll need to find a way to clean up the splatter pattern your baby will leave on the floor. Cut a shower curtain in half and place one half of it under the high chair before meals.

Never Force It. For the first few months, these feedings are more about the mealtime ritual than actually getting food down. His nutrition and calories are still coming from milk or formula. So if your baby's not interested, try again tomorrow. The worst thing you can do is teach him to dread feeding time.

Plan a Strategy. Some people start with vegetables, because they figure that once the baby tastes the sugars in fruit, he won't settle for anything else. Others feel that it's best to start off with a food that has a high likelihood of success. You make the call.

Try a Naked Lunch. Strip the baby down to his diaper before meals, and let him get as messy as he wants. When he's finished, just put him in the tub. Or better yet, feed him in the tub. Let him make his own soup.

Open Sesame. There are many ways to coerce your baby to open his mouth. Try making him smile by singing, making faces, or by feeding him with the other end of the spoon clenched between your teeth. Also, if you open your mouth as you bring the spoon to his lips, he may imitate you. (Many dads start to do this unconsciously and continue through toddlerhood.)

Choose Your Spoon Wisely. A baby spoon with a shallow trough is easier to use as a spackling tool, which is what you'll need as you continuously scrape the food from his chin back into his mouth. And always have an extra spoon on hand to give the baby in case he tries to commandeer yours. There is a wide variety of spoons in the shape of airplanes, cartoon characters, sports teams, and there are even spoons that change color when the food is too hot.

Some good choices for first foods are:

Rice cereal	**Sweet potato**	**Peas**
Barley cereal	**Carrots**	**Sweet peas**
Oat cereal	**Green beans**	**Avocado**
Squash		**Yogurt**

Serve an Appetizer. Time solid foods when the baby is not too hungry or too full. If he's too hungry, he may have no tolerance, and if he's too full, he may be disinterested or sleepy. Offer a small amount of milk right before a round of solids.

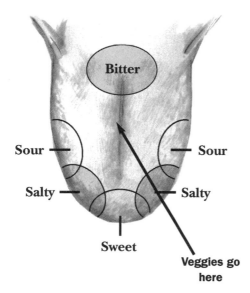

Bitter

Sour — — Sour

Salty — — Salty

Sweet

Veggies go here

When serving fruits, aim for the front of the tongue, where the tastebuds for sweetness are located. When serving vegetables, aim for the middle of the tongue, where the tastebuds are neutral.

Applesauce   Apricots

Bananas   Peaches

Prunes   Pears

CONSTIPATION

Once he starts on solids, stool production goes down but the density of each stool goes way up. Although it's best to have him making daily deposits, it's not uncommon for some babies to go three or four days without an offering. And as long as your baby seems comfortable, that's not a problem. But if you see that he is straining really hard, is in obvious discomfort, or is passing dry, hard stools, then chances are he's constipated.

Here are three ways to rectify the situation:

1. **The Four Ps** Giving your baby prunes, plums, pears, and peaches, in either fruit or juice form, can have a laxative effect.

2. **Filling the Tub** Place the baby in a warm bath. Make sure the water is up to around chest level. Now, while holding him steady with one hand, gently massage his abdomen with the other. In most cases, it won't take more than a minute or two for the baby to uncork, but it will take you much longer to clean him off and decontaminate the area.

3. **The Exersaucer** Not only is the exersaucer a favorite toy for babies this age, but the apparatus gives the baby a unique position from which to push, allowing his feet to be planted on the ground and his hands to brace against the rim. Although it doesn't have the same effect on every baby, many dads have noted the magical poop-inducing effects of the exersaucer.

If constipation persists, consult your pediatrician for more options.

Effective Diaper Disposal

A couple of years ago, if someone had told you that you would be collecting and storing human waste in your house for days at a time without dumping it outside, you may have thought them insane. Granted, it's nearly impossible to run outside every time the baby fills a diaper; so many people rely on diaper disposal units. But the most popular brands are bulky, expensive, and may require special refills. And emptying the pail is a grisly process reminiscent of that scene in *Jaws* where they slice open the dead shark's belly and remove its innards.

And because plastic is gas permeable, they don't hold in the smell. Like air slowly leaking out of a balloon, odor will eventually seep out into the atmosphere and create that distinctive "house-with-a-new-baby smell"—a combination of dirty diapers and a bunch of scents trying in vain to mask them.

As your baby gets older, and the waste becomes solid, you can dump it in the toilet, but until then, try implementing the process we call "Bag and Drop." You'll be using plain old plastic grocery bags, so you'll be recycling. And you'll be saving the dump from another unwieldy diaper pail and all those refills. This should make you feel a little less guilty about using disposables.

Step #1
Fold the scat diaper into a ball and secure with the tabs.

Step #2
Put your hand all the way inside the bag and use it to grab the diaper.

Step #3
Pull your hand back through, so the diaper is now inside the bag.

Step #4
Squeeze the air out of the bag, cinch it right above the diaper, and twist it around one rotation.

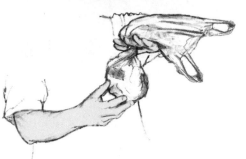

Step #5
Now put your hand inside the remaining length of the bag, grab the diaper from within, and pull your hand back through.

Step #6
Repeat step #4.

Step #7
Tie a knot in the bag. You now have two-ply odor protection. But remember, plastic is gas permeable, so we proceed to . . .

THE DROP

Place one of your large outdoor trash cans under the window of the baby's room. (If you live in a city, you can hang a bag from the rail of your fire escape.) Each time you get a dirty diaper, simply open the window and throw down a long-range jumper. Once a day, you can go out and collect the air balls, but you'll be surprised how fast you'll get your rhythm down. At the end of the week when you take out the garbage, just bring the diaper can with it.

And if you use cloth diapers, more power to you, but you've got your own waste disposal issues to deal with.

THE CLAW

A Variation on the Arcade Crane Game

Babies at 4–6 months are starting to grasp objects, and here's a fun way to sharpen their skills. Place a bunch of toys on the floor, and hold your tyke facedown on your forearm (see illustration). Make robot noises as you move him into position over the pile. When he's hovering directly above the toys, lower him onto the pile (bending from the knees), wait five seconds, and then slowly lift him up again. If he comes up with anything, shout "We have a winner!"

This exercise builds eye-hand coordination, depth perception, and fine motor skills.

FLASHLIGHT ANIMAL THEATER

Lie down with the baby in the crook of your arm and turn out the lights. Shine a flashlight on the wall. That alone will get the baby's attention. Then, assuming you're not adept at animal shadows, get some flat animal shapes—pop-outs from the little foam books, the sticky bathtub shapes, refrigerator magnets, etc.—and put them in front of the flashlight. Move them closer and the projected image becomes larger, further away and it gets smaller. Name each creature and make appropriate animal sounds.

This exercise builds visual discrimination, depth perception, and helps with language development.

If you're having trouble finding animal shapes, you can print out cut-outs from www.beprepared.net.

BABY BALLOONIST

Tie a Mylar balloon loosely to the baby's ankle. The baby will stare at the balloon intently for a while, and probably get excited. Excitement will lead to kicking, which, in turn, will cause the balloon to bob and jerk. Sooner or later, the baby will begin to understand and appreciate this cause-and-effect relationship.

This exercise builds eye-foot coordination, reasoning skills, and body awareness.

Always supervise the baby during this exercise. And never use rubber or latex balloons, because if they pop, the little bits of rubber can be choking hazards.

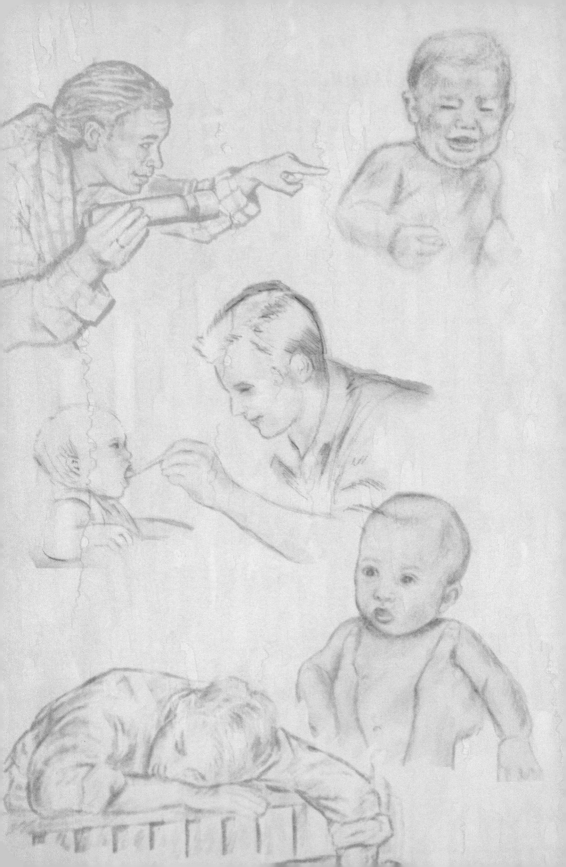

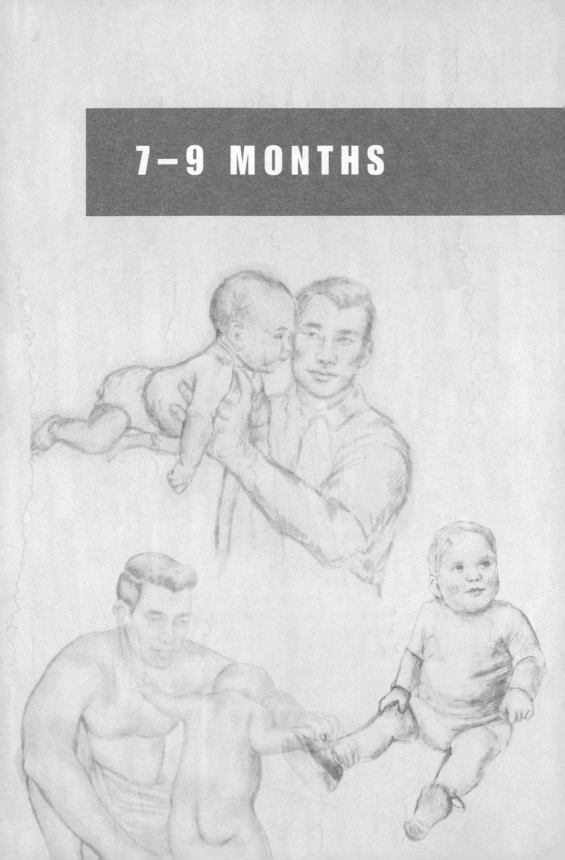

7-9 MONTHS

SLEEPING
Through the Night

Now that your baby's stomach capacity is larger she no longer needs night feedings, which was the principal reason she woke in the first place. So you and your partner will finally be able to get a full night's sleep, right?

Wrong. Most babies still wake up several times during the night. A recent survey by the National Sleep Foundation found that 76% of parents reported frequent sleep problems. So if you are among the 76%, remember that you're not alone, and if you're among the 24%, don't gloat about it, or you'll incite the wrath of the cranky majority.

Here you'll find four tactics for helping your little insomniac get to sleep and stay asleep.

1. Become a Drill Sergeant.

If you work during the day and your partner stays home, chances are you'll be in charge of bedtime routine. Many dads find this annoying, because after eight hours away from her, your natural instinct is to rile her up with some impromptu baby wrestling.

But the bedtime shift can be fun, in a mellow, Mr. Rogers–like sense. It doesn't really matter what activities you choose for your nightly routine, as long as they meet these three criteria:

1. **They are soothing.**
2. **You stick with the same activities in the same order every night.**
3. **You save the most sleep-inducing activities, such as giving the bottle, for last.**

Remember that babies, like senior citizens, thrive on routine. They take comfort in repetitive daily patterns, and will usually put up less resistance if they know what's expected of them.

2. Create a Field of Pacifiers.

If your baby uses a pacifier to fall asleep, odds are it falls out in the middle of the night and she wakes up trying to find it. To solve

this problem, liberally sprinkle pacifiers around the perimeter of the crib. Don't put them right next to her, because she may roll over on one and awaken. But if you place them around the outside, she'll eventually realize that she can always reach over to the edge and find one.

And if you have less than a dozen pacifiers in your home, you are asking for trouble. Pacifiers rival socks and umbrellas for the title of "Items That Vanish into Thin Air Most Often." If you can buy them in bulk, do so. You won't regret it.

3. Load Her Up.

Right before bed, it's a good idea to load up the baby with as much milk as she can hold. If she gets drowsy mid-feed, don't be afraid to gently jostle her to see if you can top her off. Those extra few ounces may just buy you a couple of extra hours of slumber. But try to follow it up with a quick tooth cleaning or a sip of water to rinse out the milk before she falls off.

This feeding is important because babies this age spend a lot of their time learning and honing new skills, and may not be as interested in feeding during the day.

4. Encourage Her Obsessions.

Your baby may start to form an emotional attachment to an inanimate object—a blanket, stuffed animal, or one of your or your partner's T-shirts (because of the smell) or underwear (despite the smell), especially if they are silk. (If the baby chooses a T-shirt, tie it in a knot so it won't wrap around her head.)

Her obsession with this "transitional object" is generally regarded as a healthy one, and provides fringe benefits for the whole family. Because holding her new pal gives her comfort, it becomes easier to put her into her crib at night or leave her sight for three seconds.

Some things to keep in mind:

- Steer her toward something that is easily replaceable, like an Elmo doll, rather than a hard-to-find item, like a 1986 Boston Red Sox American League Champs felt pennant.

- Try leaving the object in her crib, and when bedtime rolls around, say, "I think I hear Mr. Boxer Shorts calling you."

- If her object of choice is mass produced, go out and buy five of them, just so you don't end up driving around all night searching the streets for Tinky Winky.

If she gets attached to any object, try to buy extras.

GOING COLD TURKEY

The cold turkey method of sleep inducement is not for the faint of heart. It involves letting the baby cry in her crib for extended periods of time while you wait out in the hallway biting on a piece of rawhide.

If it didn't work, no one would do it. But many parents swear by this method, claiming that their baby now sleeps through the night. These parents are also quick to point out that the self-inflicted trauma was almost unbearable.

Once your baby is six months old, you can give this method the good old college try. Here's what you have to do:

1. Put your baby in the crib when she is drowsy but not yet asleep.

2. Leave the room.

3. No matter how hard she cries, wait five minutes.

4. Enter the room, but don't pick her up. You can put a hand on her chest or talk softly to her for thirty seconds. Reassure her that you're not Dad's evil twin.

5. Leave the room.

6. Wait five minutes.

7. Repeat this pattern until she has fallen asleep.

8. The next night do the same thing, but add another five minutes to your response time.

Within 3–5 days your baby should be able to fall asleep by herself and get herself back to sleep when she wakes up in the middle of the night.

Some things to keep in mind before trying this approach:

- Chances are that you'll be elected the torturer of your household, especially if your partner is breastfeeding, as the crying can trigger her milk flow. So she may retire to the basement, Walkman cranked up, while you're upstairs getting your game face on.

- Although your baby will cry harder than you ever thought possible (sometimes so hard that they vomit), pediatricians will assure you that no long-term emotional harm will be done to your baby. You, however, may experience flashbacks.

- Cold turkey does not work on all babies, so if it doesn't work after ten days, you may want to try something else.

- Even if it works, it can become easily undone by illness, teething, visiting grandparents, and a host of other forces beyond your control. If this happens, you'll have to start all over again.

For more information about the psychology behind the cold turkey method and other methods like it, read Solve Your Child's Sleep Problems *by Dr. Richard Ferber.*

How to Deal with 4 a.m. Wake-Ups

When your baby's cry wakes you up from a sound sleep, what do you do? If you're like most dads, you'll pretend not to hear it, hoping that your partner will respond. Your partner no doubt is employing the same tactic. And believe it or not, both of you are doing the right thing. The best way to deal with a crying seven- to nine-month-old in the middle of the night is to wait and see if she can fall back to sleep on her own.

Believe it or not, babies often practice their new skills half-asleep in their cribs. You may see your little gymnast rocking back and forth on her hands and knees or rolling around semi-conscious in the crib. It's like Cirque de Bébé in there. She may cry, grunt, whimper, and eventually fall back to sleep. So before you go in, wait a minute or two. (Obviously, if it's a pain or distress cry, go in immediately.)

When you do go in:

- Keep the lights low. In lieu of night vision glasses, you can install a red bulb in a table lamp or night light so her room will remain dark but you'll still be able to see what's going on.

- Don't smile or frown, and try to make as little eye contact as possible. Try to be monotonous, which shouldn't be hard under the circumstances.

- If she wakes demanding a bottle, it could be simply out of habit. Give her a bottle filled with water. After a couple of nights she may lose interest.

Installing a red light in your baby's lamp will allow you to see what's going on without making her think it's wake-up time. You also get that creepy Mexican bordello effect.

GOING MOBILE

A baby's first crawl is a proud moment for a new dad. All of a sudden she's in control of her own destiny, and can go wherever she wants. Basically, she's just gotten her first set of wheels.

And that first set of wheels isn't always pretty. While many babies adopt the traditional crawl, plenty of others find their own, often unorthodox methods of locomotion. Some slither on their bellies, others shuffle on their butts, and still others simply roll from place to place. If you have one of these rebel crawlers, don't worry. It's not the method that's important, it's the fact that she's learning to get around that matters.

Most babies learn to crawl between six and ten months, and usually by a year almost all are at least somewhat mobile. If your baby props herself up on her hands and knees and rocks back and forth, she's ready for take-off. You can assist by:

- modeling a crawl for her,

- letting her feet push against your hands, propelling her forward,

- putting a favorite toy just out of her reach,

- protecting your baby's knees from hard floors and rug burns by cutting the toe area off a pair of your old socks and sticking them over her legs.

And once she's got the basics down, you can create an obstacle course made up of couch cushions, phone books, and empty shoe boxes to improve her agility and maneuverability.

Expert crawlers have been clocked at speeds of up to 2 miles per hour and have been known to cover as much as 250 yards in a single day (your mileage may vary).

Yet another use for your old socks: baby kneepads

Your baby may use any number of methods of transport, including:

The Commando ────────────────
slithering on stomach using elbows
and knees to propel forward

──────────── The Naked Ape ──────────

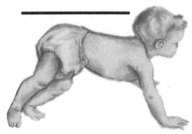

walking forward on hands and feet,
rear lifted off the ground

The Sit 'n' Slide ──────────────────
from a seated position, using hands to
drive rear end forward

─────────────── The Low Roller ──────────

lying down and rolling from place
to place, picking up crumbs and
dust balls along the way

The Jackknife ─────────────────
one leg shooting out to the side,
and the other remaining under
baby—baby tends to go in circles

BABY PROOFING

As soon as your baby becomes mobile, you come to the realization that she doesn't possess the greatest survival instincts. If anything, it seems like she's bent on self-destruction. If there is a staircase, she will attempt to fling herself down it; if there is an outlet, she will try to stick something into it; and if there's an inch of water anywhere, she will try to lie in it, facedown. It's like she's auditioning for some baby version of *Jackass*.

Since you are most likely the one with the tools, the job of babyproofing your home will most likely fall on your shoulders.

Here's a good way to start:

1. Secure a pad and a pencil;

2. get down on your hands and your knees; and

3. crawl around your house, thinking of all the ways you could possibly hurt yourself along the way and writing them down. Don't be lazy. Crawl under tables and behind the drapes, or you could miss things like exposed nails, loose change, and latches that could close on your baby's fingers.

If you're not the hands-and-knees type, and you've got some extra cash on hand, you can always pay a professional babyproofer to do the job for you. But be warned: you'll likely be told that your house is a giant death trap, and that your baby doesn't stand a chance unless you purchase a wide array of devices that just happen to be in the babyproofer's trunk.

Keep in mind that there is such a thing as too much babyproofing. If you turn your entire home into a giant playpen, your baby will have trouble learning self-control, especially when you take her to other people's homes or stores.

And the truth is that no matter how many gadgets you install, you still have to watch your baby. The day you get cocky and stop being vigilant is the day she pulls the little plastic tip off the door stopper and tries to eat it. (You need to glue it on or buy a one-piece stopper.)

If, after reading the following pages, you'd like to delve deeper, you can look through specialty catalogs like *Safety 1st* or *Safe Beginnings,* or simply go to your nearest baby superstore and peruse the huge selection of safety-related items.

Conduct a flash-light search of all the nooks and crannies in your home.

How Many Ways Can Your Baby Injure Herself in the . . .

The baby could:

Crawl into fireplace. *Install fireplace screen.*

Knock fire tools on top of herself or try to suck on them. *Place out of reach.*

Fall on edges of glass table. *Place rubber protectors around all edges.*

Try to eat candy in dish. *Place out of reach.*

Pull sculpture on top of herself. *Place out of reach.*

Eat dirt from potted plant. *Put netting over it.*

Eat the plant, which may be poisonous. *Keep plants out of reach, know the names of all houseplants and which are poisonous.*

Stick her hand in VCR door. *Get a plastic electronics shield.*

Bang her head on the sharp edges of the two square tables. *Get corner guards.*

Can you find at least 18 hazards?

Living Room?

Pull knobs off stereo and choke. *Get a plastic electronics shield.*

Pull speakers down on herself.
   Put them out of reach or bolt them down.

Walk into sliding glass doors face-first. *Put decals on doors.*

Tangle herself in drape cords. *Wrap them so they're out of reach.*

Knock over wine glass and cut herself on broken shards.
   Place out of reach.

Knock over standing lamp. *Fasten to wall.*

Tangle herself in lamp's electrical cord. *Wrap cord.*

Shove something into outlet. *Get outlet covers.*

Fall and smack her head on hearth.
   Install a padded cushion around hearth.

How Many Ways Can Your Baby **Injure** Herself in the . . .

The baby could:

Reach up to counter and spill hot coffee on herself.
Move it out of reach.

Reach up and touch front burner or knock the pot down on herself. *Always use back burner and turn pot handles inward.*

Twist knobs and turn on gas. *Install shield or knob covers.*

Pull open the stove door. *Install appliance latch.*

Open cabinet under sink and get at cleaning products.
Install lock on cabinet.

Choke on refrigerator magnets. *Remove or place out of reach.*

Tip the chair in the foreground onto herself. *Push in all chairs.*

Can you find at least 12 hazards?

Kitchen?

Tangle herself in phone cord. *Get a cord wrap.*

Try to eat contents of trash can. *Put in locked cabinet.*

Pull down tablecloth and send bowl and glass down on top of herself. *Always use placemats instead.*

Open dishwasher and take out contents or try to eat detergent. *Install shield.*

Take food from dog's food bowl or put head into water bowl. *Keep in separate gated room. (And do the same with litter boxes.)*

Because the kitchen is probably the hardest place to keep babyproofed, you can always put up a safety gate in the doorway to bar entry.

How Many Ways Can Your Baby Injure Herself in the . . .

The baby could:

Close bathroom door on her fingers. *Place a towel over the door.*

Press knob button, locking herself in bathroom. *Install a knob cover over doorknob.*

Open toilet lid and fall into bowl. *Install a lid lock on the toilet.*

Open cabinet under the sink and get at the contents.
Install a cabinet lock.

Eat the toothpaste, which can be poisonous to small children.
Put it out of reach.

Knock hair dryer into sink or toilet, or tangle self in cord.
Place out of reach.

Can you find at least 11 hazards?

Bathroom?

Slip and fall right outside of tub. *Install no-slip bath rug. (Also, install rubber bath mat on inside of tub.)*

Bang head into tub faucet. *Install faucet shield.*

Turn knobs, releasing scalding water. *Install knob covers, turn down thermostat below 120 degrees, or install scald guard.*

Try to eat razor and shampoo on the edge of the tub. *Install rack that is placed out of reach.*

Drown in small amount of water left in tub. *Always drain water.*

To keep your baby out of the bathroom entirely, you can install a hook and eye latch high up on the outside of the door.

147

BUT WAIT, THERE'S MORE

The Home Office

- Bolt down your monitor to prevent the baby genius from pulling it on top of herself.

- Thread all of your cords through a tube so she won't use them as teethers and use a surge-protector cover.

- Get a computer guard to prevent her from shoving a slice of cheese into your disk drive or shutting your computer down before you've had a chance to save your thesis.

- Anchor all bookcases and CD stands to the wall.

- Office trash cans with staples and paper clips need to be either lockable or placed out of reach of your little ragpicker.

Staircases

- Place gates at the top and bottom of every staircase.

- Remove the bottom gate once in a while and let the baby try to climb up the first couple of stairs with you holding on to her. Put carpeting or a runner on the staircase so she won't slip.

- Crawling down the stairs will require the butt-first approach, which is counter-intuitive to her self-destructive instincts. This should wait until she's proficient at climbing up, and requires extra-careful supervision from you, and possibly a helmet.

Dads and Gates

Much of your time at home will be spent hurdling baby gates. Every phone ring is like a starting gun at the Olympics. Just remember to use extra care when negotiating these barriers, especially when you're carrying the baby. Almost every dad has a story about misjudging a gate and narrowly avoiding traction.

Toys

- Make sure that all toys are sturdy, and don't have small pieces that could break off.

- Check the eyes of stuffed animals to see if they can be easily chewed off.

- If you think a toy may be too small for the baby to play with, use a toilet paper tube as a toy tester. If the toy fits through the tube, the baby could choke on it. (And don't let her play with the toilet paper tube. She could bite off chunks.)

This is the size of the hole in a toilet paper tube. Use it for reference if you don't have a real tube handy.

1 1/2

General Safety

- Check your home for lead paint.

- Make sure all poisonous substances are kept locked away out of baby's reach.

- Install smoke alarms and fire extinguishers throughout your home and escape ladders for second-floor windows.

- Keep all emergency phone numbers easily accessible, and take an infant first-aid and CPR class.

- Never leave your baby unattended.

If all of this seems like way too much for you to handle, you can always just put your baby in a giant plastic bubble until she's eighteen. But even then you'll have to watch her. Plastic is a suffocation hazard.

Removing a Foreign
Object from the VCR

You can effectively block entry by always having a tape loaded into the unit.

For some reason, babies are drawn to VCRs. No matter how often you warn them, the lure of the little black door is too much for them.

And while playing "Bye Bye Bagel" might help build their hand-eye coordination and hone their sense of spatial relationships, it can wreak havoc on your sensitive electronic equipment.

Before you start your search-and-recover, keep in mind the following:

- Never leave a VCR plugged in while working on it.

- Never stick anything hard or sharp into the unit. You could scratch the heads located in the back (see diagram), rendering your VCR useless.

- If the object is hard to grasp, you can put double-stick tape on your finger to remove it.

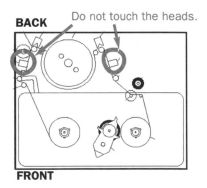

- If the object leaves any kind of residue, such as a banana, you will have to take it in for repair. Moisture in the unit will produce disastrous consequences (e.g., wads of tape wrapped around the drum and other parts of the unit, damaged heads).

- Never try to load a tape into a VCR compromised by a foreign object. This could seriously damage the loading mechanism.

150

The Terrible TUBE?

You can use the TV to put
your baby on pause.

Is it OK to let your baby watch TV? While some dads strongly
oppose the tube, most endorse any activity that enables them to
take a shower in peace.

The research on babies and TV hasn't turned up much evidence
either for or against, as it's hard to psychoanalyze a seven-month-
old. However, several years ago the AAP (American Academy of
Pediatrics) came out with a blanket statement recommending no
TV for the first two years. Their reasoning? That "babies and
toddlers have a critical need for direct interactions with parents
and other significant care givers."

This begs the question: How much direct interaction does a baby
really need? It's not like dads are throwing the baby in front of the
TV with a bottle and taking off for the weekend. But after four
hours of intense, in-your-face interaction, how much harm could
half an hour of passive staring do?

HERE ARE EIGHT ISSUES raised by the anti-TV lobby, followed by pro-moderation (sounds better than pro-TV) rebuttals.

1. **TV doesn't teach babies anything.**
   Babies commonly learn things such as songs, words, and physical skills (such as clapping or waving) from watching television. And by the way, do babies really need to be learning every second? Are they allowed any downtime?

2. **TV is bad for a baby's eyes.**
   There are no studies to prove this, and, as a matter of fact, some pediatricians have actually recommended television, and specifically sports, for the development of a baby's eye muscles. Because sports broadcasts tend to use the camera to follow a moving object—a ball, a car, a person running—they can strengthen a baby's ocular tracking muscles. (Next time your partner tells you to turn off the game, mention this fact.)

3. **TV gives babies a warped idea of reality.**
   And books don't? Have you read Mother Goose lately? The truth is, babies won't be doing any heavy thinking about reality for a while yet.

4. **The time she's watching TV is time that you could be playing with her.**
   It's also time that you could be bathing, getting something to eat, or shaking the cobwebs out of your head so that you can come back refreshed, ready for more scintillating bouts of peek-a-boo.

5. **The quick cuts and jerky camera angles will overstimulate the baby.**
   Many shows geared to babies move slowly and use smooth transitions from shot to shot. And as for broadcast TV, your baby may enjoy slow-moving fare such as C-SPAN, fishing shows, and the Weather Channel.

6. You should be reading to the baby instead.

It's true that television is no substitute for reading. Nor is it a substitute for playing or feeding or washing. Used in moderation, it's only meant to be an enjoyable complement to the daily routine.

7. Your baby will be hypnotized by the flickering demon, and will turn into a life-long addict.

Actually, many babies aren't even interested in television. And even the babies who enjoy the tube usually divide their attention between the show and all of the other fascinating colors and shapes in the room.

8. Your baby could be doing something more creative with her time.

As she gets older, your child will have the opportunity to participate in vastly more creative, interactive, and physical endeavors than television. But during these first months, there's very little she can actually do. She may show scant interest in building that model fighter jet or helping you with your taxes, but watching TV may be right up her alley.

Some quality videos for your baby to stare at:

Baby Mozart

Baby Bach

Baby Van Gogh

The Teletubbies Series

Sesame Street's *Sing Yourself Silly*

Sesame Street's *Elmo's World Series*

Hap Palmer's *Baby Songs*

Raffi in Concert

The Wiggles Series

Singing Babies—Nursery Rhyme Time

Baby Faces

Baby Know-It-All Smartypants

Baby Know-It-All Lil' Bloomer

Baby Animals: On the Farm

Babies also respond to Barney, though many dads don't have the stomach for it.

GREAT OUTINGS
7–9 Months

Your whippersnapper is becoming highly social, and wants to be included in your interactions with others. She's also entering the perpetual motion stage. Good outings for babies at this stage include:

Race Track

A stimulating trip for both dad and baby. You can cheer your picks, visit the horses in the paddock, and rip up your tickets and have the baby help you throw them in the air. It's best to go on an off day, so you can get a good view of the action without having to fight the crowds. But remember: Just because your baby likes the race track doesn't mean she'll like OTB.

Bookstore

A bookstore is a great place for babies because it's just like a library but you don't have to be quiet. Most are carpeted, so beginning crawlers can scoot through the aisles. And they have books, too.

Car Wash

The rushing water and spinning brushes of the car wash can provide a great sensory experience for babies. Before you enter, give her cues that this is going to be a safe, fun experience for the both of you. Say, "Look—the car is taking a bath!"

Laundromat

Even if you have a washing machine at home, bring a load down to the local Laundromat just so you and the baby can sit and watch your clothes dance through that little window. You can also play with her on top of the folding tables, talk to your fellow launderers, and put the baby in the laundry cart, hang a sheet from the hook at the top, and pretend she's sailing the seven seas (while holding on to her of course).

Dog Run

Although it might not be a good idea to go inside the dog run, watching from right outside the fence will usually engage your baby. Some dog runs have special areas for small dogs, where you can safely enter and watch all of the pint-size action up close.

SKILL BUILDERS
7–9 Months

Three-Cup Monte

This is a baby-friendly version of the old street scam. Start off with three large cups and a ball or small stuffed animal. You're the "tosser" and the baby is your "mark." Lift all of the cups so she can see where the object is, and then lower them all. If she chooses the right cup, she wins. And when she starts becoming consistent, slowly jockey the cups around.

Builds visual memory, problem-solving skills, and helps develop the concept of object permanence—the fact that objects exist even though she can't see them.

The Culinary Arts

Encourage your baby's burgeoning artistic skills and introduce her to new foods at the same time. Fill several plastic containers with baby foods of different colors. Put them in front of the baby and have her fingerpaint the tray of her high chair or the kitchen table. Some good baby foods to use are apples, prunes, green beans, and, for texture, vegetable rice pilaf. She can create an abstract masterpiece and safely eat the results. (You can also use four bowls of mashed potatoes and some vegetable food coloring.)

This activity is best done right before bath time.

Builds creativity, fine motor skills, and hand-eye coordination.

The Basket Train

Sit the baby in a laundry basket with a blanket or pillow against her back. Fill the rest of the basket with stuffed animals and toys, and push it around the house, simulating train noises. At various points along the way, announce stops where you drop off and pick up creatures. Eventually the baby will anticipate each stop where she can throw some animals out and invite some into her train. This game takes no small degree of exertion on your part, but the baby's excitement will hopefully energize you.

To save on back strain, you can attach a dog leash to the basket and slowly pull her around.

Builds sequential thinking and role-playing skills.

Babies and LANGUAGE

No need to order a paternity test. Your baby may call all men "dada" for a while.

You may have noticed that your baby seems more interested in what you have to say these days. A couple of months ago, your explanation of the infield fly rule would have been met with a blank stare. But now the thick fog behind her eyes is starting to disappear, giving way to a wonderfully perplexed expression. She's attempting to unravel the mysteries of language, and you are lucky enough to be able to shepherd her through this amazing and often hilarious journey.

On average, babies say their first words somewhere between 7 and 11 months. Your imp has probably started babbling, and may have even said "dada," much to your partner's chagrin. Don't tell your partner this, but "dada" is one of the most common babbling syllable combos, and is just as likely to be directed at the family dog as your face. In order for it to be considered a true first word, it needs to be said in context three times. So unless she's said "dada" three times while looking at you or your picture, it's not official. And don't be alarmed if she soon starts to refer to all men as "dada." Babies learn in categories.

vacuum

dog

truck

record

pickle

funny glasses

Babies can understand language much earlier than they'll be able to speak it effectively. Part of this is because their speech apparatus have just begun to develop, and won't be similar to an adult's until they reach six years old.

You can help your baby to speak and understand language by practicing the following:

Spark Dialogue

When you hear your baby babbling, join in as if you knew what she was talking about. After she finishes a spurt of random syllables, say, "Yeeees, that's true, but how will that affect the overseas markets?" And then wait for a response. Pretty soon she'll start to figure out the back and forth nature of true conversation. Remember to always praise her utterances, no matter how economically unsound.

Label Everything

As an everyday ritual, walk around the house with the baby, naming everything as you go. You can use it as a passive-aggressive exercise. "See? This is a gui-tar. Gui-tar. Daddy used to play this guitar every day, before you came along. And these are Rollerblades. Rol-ler-blades. Daddy used to Rollerblade all over town, before you came along." As long as you keep smiling, baby will be none the wiser.

When labeling, try not to be too general or specific. A guitar is a guitar, not an instrument (too general) or a Fender Strat-o-Caster (too specific).

Rhyme It

Research has shown that simple rhythm and rhyme is one of the best ways for children to learn language. Try reciting some Mother Goose standards, emphasizing and elongating the rhyming words. When you get bored, sing your favorite songs a cappella or create impromptu poems and limericks. But resist any references to "The Man from Nantucket," because you never know when they'll start repeating things.

Applaud All Sounds

When the baby points to the dog and says "dada," act very excited. She's starting to pair words with objects, and needs to be encouraged. Say, "Yes, that's a doggie! Doggie. Great job!" (Putting an -ie on the end of words supposedly makes it easier for babies to distinguish them.)

Chew on Some Books

Interactive books—lift-the-flap books, books with zippers and buttons, touch-and-feel books—not only build her vocabulary, but also help with hand-eye coordination and fine motor skills.

And remember, there's no wrong way to read with a baby. As long as she is enjoying herself, it doesn't matter if she wants to read the same book over and over, flip each page back and forth a hundred times, or chew on one book as you're reading another. Just relax and take comfort in the fact that she's getting an early taste for literature.

Here's a surefire way to spark your baby's book-loving instincts. Take one of your copies of *Goodnight Moon* (you'll no doubt be receiving three or four), cut out pictures of various family members, and tape them into the book. Then alter the words appropriately. "Goodnight house, and goodnight mouse, and goodnight Papa Neil, and goodnight Grandpa George."

The Secret Meaning of PEEK-A-BOO

Your baby's mind works in strange and screwy ways. Would you believe that whenever you step out of her field of vision, she thinks that you no longer exist? It's true. And for some reason, she isn't bothered by this. She just goes on playing or staring into space until you miraculously reappear. Every toy she drops, every pacifier she throws, every person who wanders out of view, ceases to exist as far as she is concerned.

Over the next few months the concept of object permanence, the idea that something exists even though she can't see it, will slowly start to take hold. Dads can help solidify this skill by:

- playing peek-a-boo,

- hiding a toy under a napkin and letting her unveil it,

- showing her the object she just dropped on the ground before picking it up.

Keep in mind that now that she's beginning to understand that you are always somewhere, and that you can always be reached, she'll start to become anxious the minute you leave the room.

When you play peek-a-boo with babies, they think that your head literally disappears and then suddenly reappears when you open your hands. No wonder they are so impressed.

Dealing with Baby Anxiety

Why shouldn't your baby have anxiety just like the rest of us? With the onset of object permanence comes **separation anxiety,** the fear of separation from you or your partner, no matter who you leave the baby with, and **stranger anxiety,** a fear of strangers, and by "strangers" we mean everyone besides you and your partner.

Some ways to deal with an anxious baby:

- Have visitors, including close relatives, approach the baby slowly, quietly, and with no sudden movements, the way you would advance toward a live grenade or homicidal maniac.

- If you are starting in a new babysitter or day care situation, stay with the baby for at least the first couple of visits, and let her see you hanging out with the caretakers.

- Babies, like dogs, have no sense of time. For your first couple of outings, come back after fifteen or twenty minutes, just to let her know that you're not fleeing the country.

- Never sneak out on your baby. You'll just reinforce the anxiety. Instead, look her in the eye, smile, and act as if it's no big deal. And NEVER go back in after you've left. Call home on your cell phone ten minutes later to make sure she stopped crying.

Believe it or not, the development of separation and stranger anxiety is a good thing. It means that you have done your job as a dad. Your baby turns to you for safety and protection.

THE BIG BATH

As soon as your baby has trouble fitting in her infant tub, it's time to upgrade her to the ultra-roomy adult bathtub. Though she may resist the change to the big tub, you can help her adjust. Try putting her into the tub with no water for the first couple of outings. Climb in with a bunch of toys and show her a good time.

Once she gets comfortable in the tub, chances are she won't want to leave. The prepared dad can use this to his advantage. The tub is an optimal place to feed her, give her medicine, and cut her nails. Pretty much anything you can do on dry land you can do in the tub, with better slop control.

Prepping for the Big Bath

1. Install a bath mat to prevent slippage.

2. Buy or create a spout cover, so the baby won't whack her head on the edge of the spout. You can make a temporary one with duct tape and a sponge.

3. Fill up the tub with three to four inches of water. Remember, babies like baths almost as warm as adults do. Use the elbow test to make sure the temperature's right.

4. Have all of your supplies at hand, including a large plastic cup, baby soap and shampoo, a washcloth, and a towel.

Jumping In

There's no better time to play with baby than when taking a bath together. Why sit hunched over the tub holding her when there's fun to be had right inside? Not only will she be enthralled by your demonstration of fluid dynamics, but she'll feel more comfortable and secure with you in the tub.

Before you get your feet wet, be sure that you're prepared for:

Getting the baby into and out of the tub. The safest way to do this is to put her on a towel on top of a curved changing pad on the floor, get in the tub by yourself, sit down, and then bring her in with you. When getting out, put the baby back on the changing pad, get out by yourself, and then pick her up.

The mid-bath movement. Your baby is likely to drop a load in the bathtub at some point. In anticipation of this event, it's a good idea to have a second large cup on hand to scoop up the scat as quickly as possible so you won't have to empty the tub and start over. If you can catch it before it hits the water, that's worth 10 points.

You'll know she's ready to launch when her body suddenly tenses up, her face turns red, and she grimaces.

If you catch it in mid-air, it's worth 10 points.

Rinsing out the hair. To avoid getting soap in your baby's eyes when you rinse her hair, stick a suction cup toy to your forehead. While the baby tilts her head back to look at the odd spectacle, rinse her hair. If your forehead won't hold a suction cup, putting a toy in your mouth and grunting may achieve similar results.

You can also try sticking a large mobile or some large plastic-coated pictures on the ceiling over the tub, then telling her to look up right before you rinse.

Another idea: If your baby has a high tolerance for head gear, you can buy a bath visor made specifically for this purpose.

For the Landlubbers

A bath seat can hold the baby upright and in place.

If you'd prefer to stay dry during the bath-time routine, you'll be needing some support keeping the baby upright. There are special apparatus created for this very purpose, and others that you can modify to suit this aim. (But remember, you still can never leave the baby in the bath unattended.)

Inflatable tub. It's a small tub that fits inside of your bathtub. It supports the baby's back, and requires less water than the big tub. Also, bath toys stay within reach.

Bath seat. Held into place with suction cups, bath seats help keep the baby upright while providing you access to wash her body.

Laundry basket. You can bathe your baby in a short plastic laundry basket with a washcloth in the bottom. The basket supports the baby's back, and water flows freely through the holes. The toys stay within reach, and when you are finished with the bath, just drain the tub and store the toys in the basket.

Tub Toys

The resourceful dad needn't go out and buy toys for the bath.
Anything in your house that floats (or sinks, for that matter)
is a potential tub toy. Some suggestions are as follows:

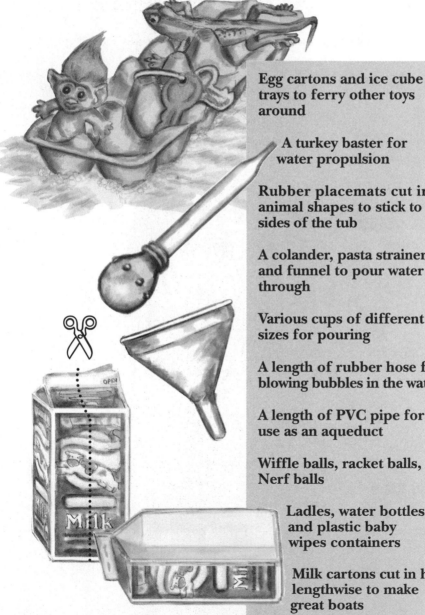

Egg cartons and ice cube trays to ferry other toys around

A turkey baster for water propulsion

Rubber placemats cut into animal shapes to stick to the sides of the tub

A colander, pasta strainer, and funnel to pour water through

Various cups of different sizes for pouring

A length of rubber hose for blowing bubbles in the water

A length of PVC pipe for use as an aqueduct

Wiffle balls, racket balls, Nerf balls

Ladles, water bottles, and plastic baby wipes containers

Milk cartons cut in half lengthwise to make great boats

FIRST Haircut

The only real reason to give a baby a haircut during the first year is maintenance—either the bangs are interfering with her vision or the back is growing long enough to be mistaken for a mullet. In either case, action must be taken.

Your partner may suggest one of the many child-friendly styling salons—something with a name like ShortCutz, Clips 'n' Giggles, or Hairy Potter's. But if you want to save some time and money and possibly alleviate a crying fit, you can do it yourself.

If you are at all apprehensive at the prospect of cutting a baby's hair, realize that no matter how badly you botch the job (short of drawing blood), your baby will still look cute.

Cutting the Back

Place your awake baby in her high chair in front of the TV. (If you don't let the baby watch TV, your partner will have to do a puppet show.) Stand behind the baby, and using your rounded scissors, cut from the center out in both directions. Cut small amounts at a time so you can easily cover up errors.

Cutting the Bangs

Because babies will often flail their arms and whip their heads around to get away from a scissors approaching their faces (a very good instinct in most situations), it's best to cut a baby's bangs when she is sound asleep, preferably sitting up in the stroller or car seat so you can get a good angle. Make sure to use the scissors with the rounded edges, and always have your fingers in between the scissors and the baby's head (see below).

NAIL CARE

Because of the surgical precision involved, many dads get unwillingly recruited into nail duty. Your partner may figure, "If you can bait a hook, you can cut a fingernail."

If your baby's a heavy sleeper, you can do it then. Otherwise, you'll either need an assistant to hold her hand still or a very engaging distraction, such as a favorite video, to keep her busy. Some dads do it right after a bath, when the nails are especially pliable.

When cutting, you can use either a pair of baby nail scissors with the rounded tips, or blunt-edged nose-hair scissors, which some dads say are even easier to maneuver. And don't worry if you draw a little bit of blood. It happens to almost everybody, especially the first few times out. To minimize the chance of catching skin, press the fleshy part of the finger down as you cut.

10–12 MONTHS

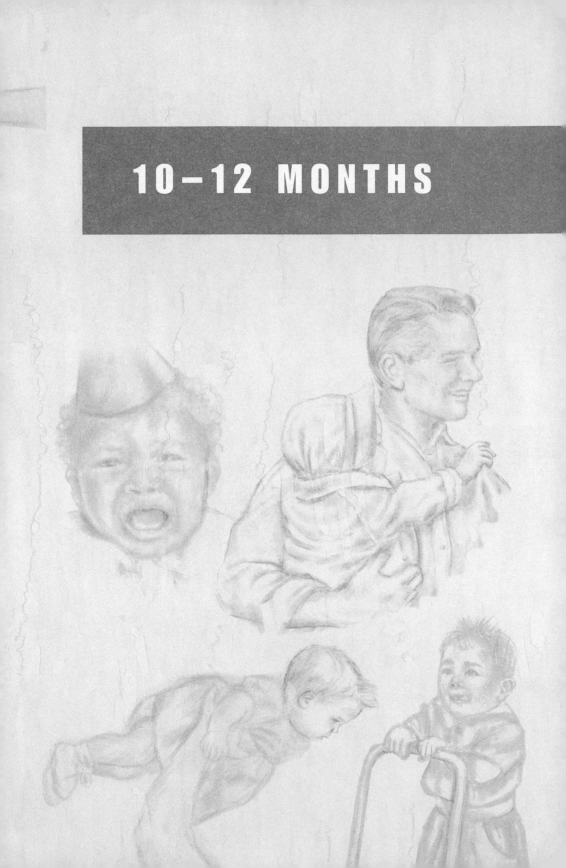

EATING Like a Person

When you started your baby on solids, did you stop and think about how unsolid those foods were? Everything is pretty much the same consistency—mush. Well, by 10–12 months many babies rebel against the mush and start craving finger foods more and more. They look at the various shades of brownish slop on their plate, and then the burger and fries on your plate, and you can't blame them for trying to fling themselves out of their high chairs in protest.

Not to mention the fact that the store-bought baby foods created for the ten- to twelve-month-old market are suspect, to say the least. Would you eat a jar of orange-colored paste labeled Pears and Chicken? What about an inky gel that goes by the name Blueberry Buckle? And consider, if you will, Turkey, Rice, and Garden Vegetables. Can they take an entire three-course meal and cram it into a tiny jar? Is that even legal?

It's definitely time to make finger foods a more visible part of your baby's mealtime. They are easy to prepare, there's plenty of variety, and you don't have to worry about running out of those suspicious little jars. And not only will your baby relish the independence of controlling his own food intake, he'll also be developing his pincer grasp, squeezing together his thumb and forefinger in order to pick things up.

Can a three-course meal be crammed into a tiny jar?

Here are some things to keep in mind when offering finger foods:

Keep the pieces small. When serving finger foods, make sure to keep the individual pieces to about the size of a Cheerio. Anything larger could be a choking hazard.

Finger foods give your baby a chance to develop his pincer grasp.

Have patience. It will take time to figure out the culinary particulars of your squirt. Let him experiment with a wide variety of flavors and textures, and see which ones he gravitates toward. It may take up to ten exposures for him to decide if something gets the green light.

Put it in piles. A good way to serve finger foods is to cut up the little pieces and put them in piles on his high chair tray. If each food is in its own individual pile, he can easily access the stuff he likes and ignore the rest.

Babies need to eat less than you think. At this stage, a baby should be eating between 4 and 8 tablespoons of fruits and vegetables, 2–4 tablespoons of protein, and 8 tablespoons of rice, cereal, potatoes, or pasta (or half a slice of bread) per day. Of course, this is all supplemented by milk.

Give milk after food. At least 50% of your baby's nutrition is still coming from formula or breast milk. You'll have much more success with finger foods if you hold off on the milk until after you give him the solid stuff.

Make it interesting. Some babies are slow to adapt to finger foods, and still prefer the stuff in the jars. As with most baby-related activities, if you can make something seem exciting, your baby will be more likely to take the bait. You can make finger food more alluring by melting cheese on top of it, placing individual morsels on fanned-out measuring spoons, or covering the pile of food with a plastic cup so the baby has to lift off the cup to get at the pieces. Pretend that lifting the cup is strictly taboo.

The Sippy Cup

You are eventually going to have to phase out the bottle, and the sippy cup is a good way to start the transition to the big cup.

Because sippy cups are spill-proof, your little hellion can throw it out of his car seat with no ill effects. Some youngsters are given a regular drinking cup at this age, but very little liquid ends up in their mouths.

You can create a starter sippy cup from a baby bottle and a drinking straw. Although your baby will be learning a new way to drink, he'll still have the familiarity and comfort of his bottle.

1. Cut a small X in a baby bottle nipple. If the X is too big, it won't be leak-proof.

2. Pour your baby's liquid of choice into the bottle.

3. Place the nipple, inverted, into the bottle.

4. Screw on the ring.

5. Stick a straw through the X in the nipple.

Veggie Booty

We would only mention the brand name of a product if it's something really unique and helpful. Veggie Booty fits the bill perfectly. Picture, if you will, a cheese doodle, but instead of cheese, it contains spinach, kale, cabbage, carrots, and broccoli. And believe it or not, they don't taste half bad. And many babies go nuts for them.

Veggie Booty is carried in select supermarkets and health food stores. You can also order it online at www.robscape.com. As a snack food, they are a much better choice than pork rinds.

A List of Finger Foods
for Your Baby to Eat and Throw

Cottage cheese

Ricotta cheese

Soft, steamed carrots

Cooked poultry

Peaches

Toasted whole wheat bread
  (*without nuts*)

Bagel

Cream cheese on crackers

Avocado

Bananas

Boiled yolks
  (*but no whites until after a year*)

Dry cereal

Well-cooked pasta
  (*spirals or shell shapes*)

Yogurt

Pancakes

Breadsticks

French fries

Graham crackers

Pickles (*cut extra small*)

Macaroni and cheese

Ground beef

Tofu

Sweet potatoes

Be sure to keep the pieces no bigger than a Cheerio.

Eleven Foods You Should Never Give Your Baby

The following foods have been known to cause allergic reactions or
health problems, or are choking hazards, and should be avoided:

Honey

Cow's milk

Egg whites

Citrus fruits and juices

Peanut butter

Whole grapes

All seeds and nuts

Blueberries

Popcorn

Raw vegetables

Hot dogs

Also, limit foods high in
saturated fat, salt, or added
sugar and foods that contain
artificial sweeteners.

BABIES and Restaurants

When going out to a restaurant with your small fry, keep your expectations low. Don't expect to enjoy your meal. Don't expect to converse with your partner. And don't expect your fellow diners to be anything but irritated by your presence. And if by chance your baby is angelic, count your blessings and wolf down your meal as quickly as possible.

Of course, you should refrain from taking your baby anyplace fancy. If someone is spending $40 for an entrée the size of a hockey puck, they deserve a baby-free dining experience. But if you take the urchin to a family-style restaurant and you get dirty looks from the other patrons, then it's their problem, not yours.

How can you tell which restaurants are appropriate for babies and which aren't? Look at the lists of clues on the following page.

Babies love giant guitars.

Baby-Friendly Clues

Crayons

High chairs

Televisions

A drive-thru window

Plastic trays

Neon

"No Shirt No Shoes
No Service" sign on door

Waiters with name tags

Ketchup on the table

A man in a giant foam
mouse costume

Baby-Unfriendly Clues

Tablecloths

Candles

Those giant pepper mills

Waiters with crumbers in their
pockets

Napkins made into origami
shapes

Water served in wine glasses

The phrase "prix fixe"

More than two forks at each
place setting

A bathroom attendant

Anything served "under glass"

If you don't get the chance to case the joint, be aware that some genres of restaurants are known for being particularly conducive to family dining:

- Sports bars are good because the high noise level can mask baby cries, and the multiple televisions can keep your baby transfixed.

- Mexican restaurants are usually loud and casual, and some feature mariachi bands.

- Seafood restaurants can have fish or lobster tanks and those little oyster crackers that your munchkin can chew on.

- Chinese restaurants feature those crunchy noodles you get when you first sit down. Fried rice dishes are good for babies, and a fortune cookie, broken into little pieces and placed in a pile in front of the baby, can keep him busy for a good fifteen minutes.

- Salad bars are great because food can be on your baby's plate within thirty seconds and you can offer him a bunch of stuff from which to sample.

How to Make It Through the Meal

- **Go early.** Especially for the first couple of trials, go as early as you can. Most restaurants are pretty empty from 5:30-6:30, and if there are other patrons, they are usually senior citizens, who just may enjoy the company.

- **Pre-feed the baby.** If he's starving when you enter the restaurant, you are in for a long dinner. Feed him a bit before you go out. You can also order over the phone, and make sure the waiter brings bread and crackers as you sit down.

- **Choose your seats strategically.** The best place to sit is near an exit, so you can immediately walk out if the baby starts crying. Stay away from the kitchen, so you don't have the waiters running by with hot trays. Booths are usually a bad idea, because then the high chair will be jutting out into the aisle and blocking traffic. Putting the baby in front of a window or fish tank may help entertain him during the meal.

- **Bring activities.** Toys and books will help get him through the meal. If you forget toys, the resourceful dad can use whatever he has on hand.

  - Sugar packets can be made into impromptu rattles (just don't let him try to eat them).

  - A plastic "to go" cup with a lid on top and an ice cube inside can fascinate him for surprisingly long periods.

  - Cold spoons can be effective chew toys.

- **Take it outside.** At the first sign of tears, pick him up and go out to the parking lot. At the next outburst, have your partner go out, so both of your meals will get cold evenly. Order items that will taste good lukewarm, cold, or reheated from a to-go carton an hour later.

If you are by yourself with the baby, it's probably best to just go for pizza or order take-out.

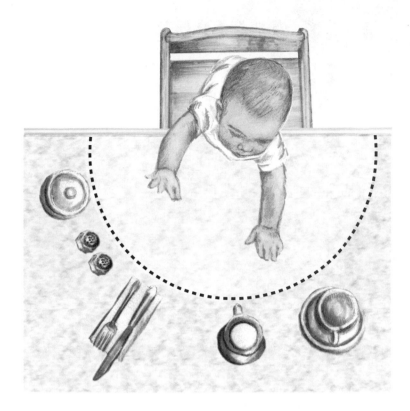

- **Create a no-fly zone.** No food or drinks of any kind should be allowed within the baby's lunge radius. At the beginning of the meal, put a toy near the center of the table to see how far your baby can fully extend his arm, and then make sure nothing except the baby's food and toys enter the zone. Many waiters, either absentmindedly or passive-aggressively, choose to put all the hottest items in front of the baby, so be sure to remind them to adhere to the no-fly zone.

- **Tip like a big shot.** If you've ever waited tables, then you know how disgusting it is to pick up piles of half-eaten mush from the floor. So before you leave, either pick up most of it yourself, or make sure to compensate your waiter for his or her troubles in the form of a big tip. And remember—your baby has taken up an adult's seat, so you can tip as if he had ordered an adult-priced meal. Your servers will remember your generosity (or lack thereof) the next time you walk in.

GREAT OUTINGS
10–12 Months

Your almost-one-year-old has had it with sitting still and staring straight ahead. He now seeks action and adventure. Some good activities for this age group include:

Construction Sites Dump trucks unloading, cranes lifting up girders, supports being driven into the ground, cement being poured and smoothed, and bricks being laid—you can't beat the sights, sounds, and smells of a construction site. And your baby may enjoy it, too.

Birthday Parties You'll no doubt be invited to birthday parties of babies born around the same time as yours, and you should take every opportunity to go. It's a painless way to spend an afternoon with your sprout. The venue will most likely be babyproofed, they'll have snacks and baby-oriented activities, and you can compare notes with other parents. Also, seeing all of those babies will help you realize how advanced yours is.

Pizza Parlor This is a great activity. You order a pizza and then watch it being kneaded, tossed, and topped. Then you can start teaching the baby about the gustatory power of pizza.

Feeding the Ducks Have the baby throw small pieces of bread to the ducks. Make sure that you're holding on to him at all times, because mallards can get a bit aggressive, and you don't want your baby having Hitchcockian duck nightmares when he grows up. If you don't live around ducks, substitute squirrels or pigeons.

Department Stores Department stores have two things going for them—they have a whole bunch of items under one roof and they are usually understaffed. The baby can start off crawling around in the carpet department, bounce on over to bedding, and when he's ready for a nap, you can find an out-of-the-way couch where you can both grab some shut-eye.

SKILL Builders
10–12 Months

Pushcart Bullfight

In this game, the baby gets to practice his walking skills and you get to brush up on your matador moves. Have him stand on one side of the room with his push-style walker, and you stand on the other waving a colorful towel or blanket. Motion the baby to come over to you with a "Toro, toro!" and when he does, swoop the towel over his head and run to the other side of the room. The baby will most likely get excited and give chase.

Builds balance, coordination, and walking skills.

Note: Push walkers are great for babies this age, but make sure to get one with a sturdy, heavy base so the baby won't topple when leaning on it.

The Dad Hammock

Lay a blanket, towel, or sheet on the floor and place the baby in the center. Grab the two corners nearest his head with one hand and the two corners nearest his feet with the other hand. Make sure you've got a tight grip, and that the baby can peek out through a crack in the center. Lift the blanket and gently swing him back and forth, being careful to avoid furniture.

If your baby is at all hesitant or skeptical about this activity, first demo it with his stuffed animals while he watches, and then ask him if he wants a turn.

Builds trust, spatial awareness, and Dad's traps and delts.

The DECOY Drawer

Your electronic gear is part of what makes you who you are. With your cell phone, beeper, PDA, and universal remote by your side, you feel a sense of oneness with the world—always reachable, never bored, confident to take on whatever adventure life, or cable, throws your way.

Somehow the baby senses the power these objects possess and will take every opportunity to seize and/or destroy them.

You decide to buy the baby colorful plastic versions of his own. That way he'll have his toys to play with, and you'll have yours. But of course the baby immediately throws aside the imposters and goes back to the genuine articles.

That's why you need to create a decoy drawer full of old phones, beepers, PDAs, and remotes, not to mention wallets, keys, credit cards, calculators, and VHS tapes. The drawer should be at a good baby height, and all items need to be real but non-functioning. That way when the baby opens the drawer, he'll think he's hit the mother lode.

You've got to sell the fake.

But this deception won't work unless you sell the fake. Every time the baby goes into the drawer, you've got to give him a look of reproach that reassures him that he's doing something strictly off-limits.

You can create a decoy drawer in almost any room in the house. It will provide hours of fun for the baby and give you some much-needed downtime.

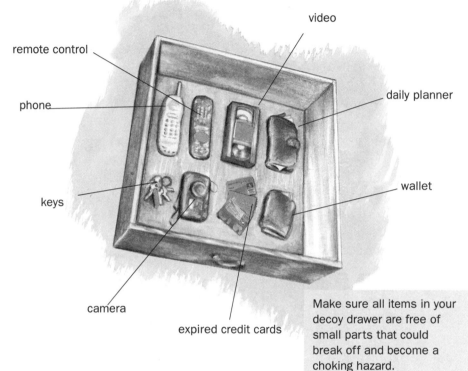

video

remote control

phone

daily planner

keys

wallet

camera

expired credit cards

Make sure all items in your decoy drawer are free of small parts that could break off and become a choking hazard.

Creating a Decoy Drawer

Kitchen Decoy Drawer
Pots and pans, plastic cups and saucers, soup containers, wooden spoons, egg cartons.

Bathroom Decoy Drawer
Old washed-out shampoo bottles, a plastic soap dish, empty Band-Aid boxes, a childproof handheld mirror.

Home-Office Decoy Drawer
Unlock one drawer of the file cabinet and fill file folders with scrap paper and junk mail. Who needs a shredder when you've got a baby in the house? (Install rubber stoppers to prevent finger slams and make sure the baby doesn't eat the paper.)

RIGGING EMERGENCY DIAPERS

It's 4 a.m. and the baby is crying. You guess it's a discomfort cry, and your theory is confirmed by the pungent smell that hits you when you enter the room. You reach into the drawer for a clean diaper and come up with—nothing. You are completely out and you are going to have to wait until morning to replenish your stock.

You assume this won't happen to you? You'll be lucky if it happens only once.

The prepared dad knows how to rig up a makeshift diaper for just such an emergency. Your homemade diaper won't need to be super-absorbent, ultra-comfortable, or aesthetically pleasing. It just needs to work well enough to get you through the night, so you can mobilize at dawn to buy some real ones.

Instructions:

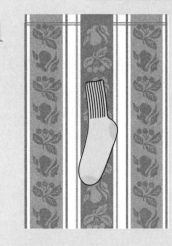

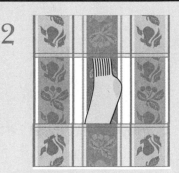

1. Lay out the dishtowel and place the sock in the center, lengthwise.

2. Fold over the sides of the dishtowel to make a square.

3. Lay baby on top of dishtowel, fold the bottom part between his legs and up so it rests on top of his midsection.

4. Tuck the front corners inside of the back corners and secure with duct tape. Make sure that it's not too tight, and that the duct tape doesn't get near the baby's skin.

What you are going to need:

1 clean dishtowel

1 clean cotton sweat sock

1 roll of duct tape

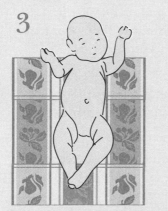

3

4

Warning: Make sure you have a pair of safety scissors on hand. Otherwise, it may be difficult to extricate the baby.

5. If diaper is too saggy in the crotch area, use extra duct tape to close the space.

6. If you want to waterproof the diaper (which is highly advisable), simply duct-tape as much of the surface area as you can, making sure that baby's skin won't be chafed.

ADVANCED
Changing Maneuvers

With older babies you have to modify your diaper-changing techniques.

The Standing Diaper Change

Obsessed with standing up, babies this age don't appreciate being forced to lie down for a diaper change. So they'll writhe around, looking for any way possible to get free of your grip, even if it means taking a header off the changing table. In these situations, the prepared dad makes use of the standing diaper change, which is meant for a urine-filled diaper, but can work for most scat diapers as well, as long as you're careful.

Procedure:

1. Pile a bunch of toys up on a couch or chair. If it's a chair, secure it in place so it won't slide around during the change.

2. Start loudly playing with the toys, luring the baby over to the staging area. If you forcibly drag him over, you'll tip your hand, and he'll know something's up.

3. Lean him up against the couch or chair. Always keep one hand on him in case he starts to tilt. Then quickly unsnap or unzip his pants legs and tuck them into the neck of his shirt to give you clear access to the diaper.

4. Act like a pit crew, changing and wiping as quickly as humanly possible. You have no idea when he'll get bored and scoot away. And more importantly, you have no idea if he's got any ammo left, so you want to severely limit the time he is bottomless.

The Standing Lap Change

The standing lap change is for those times when you can't administer the standing diaper change. If you are sitting in a crowded bus, train, or sports arena, for instance.

In this change, you remain seated while the baby stands in your lap. He's facing you, leaning on your shoulders or chest for support. The procedure is similar to the standing diaper change, but since the baby is looking directly at you, you must find a different way to keep him occupied and cooperative during the change.

If you're wearing a baseball cap, you can turn yourself into a human mobile by clipping a pacifier cord to the brim and dangling a toy from the cord.

One way to distract the baby: become a mobile.

Big League Blow-Outs

Every once in a while your baby will stun you with a volcanic liquid poop that will quickly overflow the diaper and shoot up his back. This event is known as a blow-out.

If he blows out at home, pray that he's not inhabiting your couch at the time. And if he blows out on the road, pray you've brought enough wipes to contain the mess. More than one dad has had to sacrifice his socks for the cause.

An immediate bath is the best solution. Barring that, lay the baby on a changing pad or brown towel and quickly remove his soiled clothing. Use the unsoiled areas of the clothing to mop up the mess. Throw the clothes in a plastic bag (you should have at least two or three with you at all times), and start cleaning with wipes, or a wet washcloth if you have access to one. Do a basic sweep first, and then move on to detailed cleaning once the muck is under control.

Making Your Baby LAUGH

Because babies have little control over their environment, they think it's hysterical to disrupt yours.

Just as your partner is uniquely qualified to breastfeed, you are uniquely qualified to provide comic relief for your baby. That's not saying your partner won't be able to conjure up some baby laughs. But when it comes to understanding the infant sense of humor, you've got the edge, because it's probably not that different from your own. If you've ever enjoyed The Three Stooges, Bugs Bunny, or any Mel Brooks movie, then you've got all the tools you need to create your own baby stand-up routine.

You'll discover your baby's favorite jokes through trial and error, and sometimes completely by accident. A random sneeze may trigger a belly laugh, and an apple rolling off a table may send him over the edge. But if you're ever stuck for material, here are some time-honored gags, broken down into categories, that will hopefully leave your baby drooling for more:

Dad as Baby

- Put his pacifier in your mouth backwards, try to suck on it, and then spit it out in frustration.

- While he's drinking his bottle, try to drink from the other end.

- Crawl around on the floor and have your partner chase you.

Dad as Complete Moron

- Try to put the baby's pants on your head, or the baby's shoes on the dog.

- Put a toy on your head and pretend to look for it. When it falls to the floor,act startled.

- Show him pictures of various animals but get their sounds wrong. "The cow says oink!" (Eventually he'll catch on.)

Dad as Animal

- Growl like a dog, and pull off baby's sock using only your teeth. Have him try to get the sock out of your mouth.

- Pretend that your finger is a buzzing bee and have it land first on your nose and then on baby's. Keep shooing it off.

- Pretend that one of your hands is a lobster claw and have it snap at the baby and then yourself. Have it latch on to your nose and not let go.

The Revenge of Dad

- Pretend to eat the baby like a giant ear of corn.

- Smell his feet, make a disgusted face, and push them away, saying, "Stinky feet!"

- Curl the baby like a barbell, and when he gets close to your mouth, do a giant raspberry on his stomach.

Baby Causing Pain to Dad

- Build a block tower, and when he knocks it over, cry loudly.

- Lying next to the baby, close your eyes and snore loudly. When he pokes you, lift your head up and say, "I'm trying to get some sleep around here!" and lie back down. Repeat.

- Hold a piece of the baby's food close to him, and pretend not to notice when he takes it from your hand. Then look at your empty hand and say, "Hey, that's my food!"

Dad Causing Pain to Dad

- Hit yourself in the head with an empty plastic bottle, and then imitate Homer Simpson's "Doh!"

- Trip over one of the baby's toys and do a big pratfall onto the couch.

- Hold a water pistol or spray bottle in your hand. Point it at your face, look at the trigger, and say, "I wonder what this does." Squirt yourself and scream.

A joke occurs when you expect one thing and you get something completely different. Most babies under seven or eight months old don't understand jokes, because they have no expectations. They accept everything at face value. In short, they're gullible.

BABIES and Airplanes

Let those around you share the responsibility of entertaining the baby.

Tired of spending all of your time cooped up in the house with your baby? Instead, why not spend some time cooped up in an airplane with him? If nothing else, do it for the sheer pleasure of watching all of the other passengers' terrified reactions as you and the baby board the plane and walk down the aisle toward them, looking for your seats. (For added effect, walk up and down several times before settling in.)

When traveling by plane, the most that any parent can hope for is a quiet baby. Employ the following seven tactics to pacify him in transit:

1. Choose your seats wisely.

When booking a flight, keep in mind the following:

- If you don't want to buy a seat for your baby, you and your partner should reserve the window and aisle seats in the same row, leaving the middle seat open. Middles always fill up last, and even if someone has reserved it, as soon as they see the baby they'll beg the flight attendant for reassignment.

- The bulkhead row offers the most legroom, and having a wall in front of you is a blessing, especially when the baby decides to throw his toys around. And if you put in a request, some airlines will provide bassinets that attach to the bulkhead.

- If you sit near the restroom, there's usually extra space to move around. And the near-constant flow of people may keep the baby entertained. You can play peek-a-boo with passengers as they enter and exit the restroom (whether they like it or not), and you can go into the restroom with the baby to stare in the mirror, flick the switches, and marvel at the blue water swirling down the drain.

- Parents with babies are not allowed to sit in the exit rows. Presumably this is because after an hour with a screaming baby, you might try to pull the emergency latch and jump out.

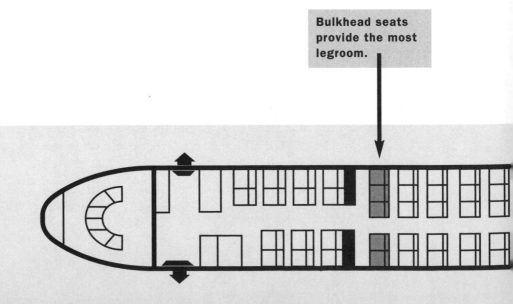

Bulkhead seats provide the most legroom.

2. Increase the odds of sleep.

Some ways to induce in-flight slumber are:

- Time your trip with his nap or suck it up and take the red-eye.

- Get to the airport early, and run him ragged. This won't be hard to do, as babies are energized by the wide-open spaces, moving walkways, and carpeted hallways of airports.

- Board last, even though you are allowed to board first. Either you or your partner board with all of the gear while the other one wears him out in the waiting area.

- Dose your baby into dreamland with baby Benadryl or Tylenol, but always consult your doctor before administering any medicine.

3. Feed during take-offs and landings.

In order to balance the pressure in your baby's ears, he should be on the breast or bottle during take-offs and especially during landings. If he's not hungry, a pacifier can also work to relieve the pressure. And if the baby refuses to suck, he'll feel pain in his ears and start crying, an activity that will also help to balance the pressure.

Seats near the bathrooms provide the best entertainment value.

If you need to heat a bottle onboard, you can ask the flight attendant to pour hot water into an air sick bag, and then you put the bottle in the bag for a few minutes.

Formula is the easiest way to feed a baby on a plane. Some dads pre-measure the powder into little plastic bags, but this might not be the best idea if you want to clear security in a timely manner.

If you were airport security and you saw this bag, what would you think?

4. Prepare for flying fluids.

Because the risk of air sickness is always high, remember to pack three or four extra outfits for him. And you should wear a windbreaker over your clothes so you can just wipe it down if you get vomited upon. Bring plastic bags, wipes, and paper towels for containment purposes.

Changing dirty diapers in a tiny airplane bathroom is almost impossible, so you may want to do it on a blanket or towel across your and your partner's laps. When finished, place the dirty diaper in an air sickness bag. And if the odor is particularly offensive, offer to buy drinks for those passengers closest to you.

When exiting the plane, it's a good idea to grab as many air sickness bags as you can carry. They are great for storing wet or dirty clothes, rancid diapers, and other baby-related debris.

5. Deploy toys at regular intervals.

Go to a second-hand store and buy a bunch of rubber and plastic toys. Sterilize them in the top rack of the dishwasher and then wrap them up in paper bags. As soon as you notice the baby getting fussy, hand him a new toy to unwrap. Figure on one toy for each half-hour of flight time. You can also buy some press-on window decals for the baby to stick to the window and peel off.

And deflated blow-up toys take up almost no space.

If you run out of toys, try making a puppet out of an air sick bag. Or have him play with the airfone on the seat back. Many babies have an obsession with tickets, so your boarding pass may also keep him busy for a while.

6. Force others to entertain the baby.

Hold him up directly in front of the passengers nearest you and see if anyone bites. If you keep him there for an uncomfortably long time, someone is bound to look up from their *Skyward* magazine and force a smile. That's when you say to the baby, "I think somebody wants to play with you." Look at it this way: if everyone wants a quiet baby, they're going to have to do their part.

7. Bring baby-holding devices.

Most airlines let you bring your small umbrella-type stroller and car seat on the plane. If the baby has his own seat, strap him into the car seat for take-off and landing. Putting him in the front carrier is also an option for take-offs and landings, and you'll still have your hands free.

Having a stroller with you at all times is important, particularly when you are stuck in an airport because your connecting flight is three hours late or you're held up waiting for dogs to come and sniff your powdered formula.

Hotel, Motel, HOLIDAY INN

It's worth staying at a hotel with your baby for the long hallways alone. Hotel hallways are to ten- to twelve-month-olds what empty swimming pools are to skateboarders: ideal places to hone their skills. The walls are smooth and even and the floors are thickly carpeted, cushioning the inevitable face plant. And every journey can end in a visit to the ice machine—an all-time baby favorite combining equal parts sight, sound, touch, and taste.

Hotels can provide a much-needed break for dads, too. It's refreshing to see your baby trashing someone else's place for once. But before turning your baby loose in his new habitat, there are two issues that you'll need to address: sleep and safety.

Hotel Sleep Solutions

- **Bring a port-a-crib.** Most hotels provide cribs, but in general they are rickety and poorly maintained, and the mattresses have seen one too many baby leakages. For peace of mind, take along your port-a-crib. And have your baby sleep in it a couple of nights before you arrive just to get him used to the change.

- **Bring bathroom activities.** This is for you, not your baby. Because once you get him to sleep, you and your partner may be stuck in the bathroom for a couple of hours. Your partner may feel that this is a perfect time to talk about your relationship. To avoid this, bring a game of Scrabble, a deck of cards, a chess board, anything to keep you both occupied.

- **Block your baby's view of the bed.** When your baby wakes up in the middle of the night and sees you in the bed right next to him, he may never get back to sleep. So you need to block his view of the bed. Put chairs in between the crib and the bed, and then place towels or extra bedding on top of the chairs.

- **Take shifts.** Just because one of you is stuck in the room with the baby doesn't mean the both of you have to suffer. Take shifts. While your partner goes down to the hotel bar to fend off conventioneers, you can hang out in the room, listen to the Walkman, read the Bible, play games on your PDA, or, if the baby permits, watch low-volume TV. After an hour or so, switch.

- **Make the room conducive to sleep.** To keep the room dark, take some hangers from the closet and use them to clamp the curtains together. And to create white noise, see if you can disconnect the cable from the back of the TV set. Then turn on the TV, and place a towel over the screen to block out the light. Or put a thin T-shirt over the screen, which will give you a glowing night-light effect.

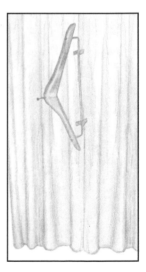

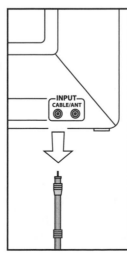

Using these two methods will help you block out both light and noise.

The Four-Minute Babyproofing

Your baby may assume the minibar is for mini-people.

Babyproofing your hotel room won't take nearly as long as babyproofing your home, and because you'll only be there for a short period of time, your installations should be fairly easy to remove. Some hotels supply childproofing kits, but most expect you to do it yourself, a feat that should take you less than five minutes. The only supplies you'll need are electrical tape (easier to remove than duct tape) and pipe cleaners.

- Before you let the baby crawl around the room, sweep the floor for hazardous items like paper clips and loose change. Place the coffeemaker, hair dryer, and iron out of reach.

- Use electrical tape to cover up outlets and tape drawers shut, and secure the minibar. To protect your baby's head from sharp corners, bring along extra baby socks, fold them in half, and tape them over all furniture corners that are at the baby's height or below.

- Tape a big X across the sliding glass doors leading to the balcony to let the baby know that he can't go straight through the doorway. And make sure those doors are locked. Use pipe cleaners to wrangle all drape and blind cords, and also to gather lamp cords. Secure closet doors by wrapping a pipe cleaner around both knobs and twisting.

- It's a good idea to keep the bathroom door closed and off-limits at all times. If your baby has figured out how to open doors, put one of your socks over the bathroom doorknob. He will have a tough time getting enough traction to open it.

Use folded baby socks as corner protectors.

Remember to tip housekeeping well. Babies can do more damage to hotel rooms than heavy metal bands, and you should compensate accordingly.

How to Neutralize
a RUNNER

Some one-year-olds walk, and others run. Undaunted by crowded aisles, steep escalators, and busy intersections, they forge ahead, like Shackleton, toward the great unknown.

As a father, you admire your baby's determination, but as a parent who wants to bring home a live child, you know you have to restrain him somehow. And the best way to deal with an AWOL threat is to outfit him in clothes that you can get a grip on, such as:

- Hooded sweatshirts

- Overalls

- Suspenders

- Pants with belt loops

Use your baby's hood as a makeshift leash.

When a potentially hazardous situation arises, just grab hold and he's immobile. (When using the hood, only use gentle tugs.) Then, when the danger passes, let go and he's once again free to taste-test every surface in the mall.

Camping with Your CUB

Your baby should not be an excuse to retire your tent and sleeping bag. On the contrary, camping with a bambino can be a great experience for the whole family. You'll get the thrill of introducing him to all the wonders of nature, and he'll have the opportunity to eat a much better variety of dirt than he gets at home.

You're going to be hauling plenty of gear, especially if you decide to go backpacking in the woods. One of you will have to carry the baby and the other will have to carry everything else. Trudging through the forest with the baby in one backpack and the mountain of equipment in the other, you may feel like Sherpa mountain guides that your baby has hired for an expedition.

Setting Up Camp

- Pick a campsite that's a good distance away from other campers. You don't want your baby's 3 a.m. screams waking up your fellow campmates. Conversely, you don't want your fellow campmates' 3 a.m. screams waking up your baby.

- You'll need something to put him in while setting up camp. If you put up your tent first, it can function as an instant playpen. But the baby may be happier in a port-a-crib. He'll be able to pull himself up and peruse the great outdoors.

- Once you're set up, put some long pants on the baby and let him crawl around the environs with you in tow. Just make sure he doesn't try to eat any plants, stick his hand down any snake holes, or crawl into the campfire. But allow him to get filthy. A layer of dirt will do him some good. It helps protect him from the sun and bugs.

- You can use baby-safe sunscreen and bug repellent on babies over six months old as long as you don't get them anywhere near the hands or eyes. And because you may encounter ticks, mosquitoes, poison ivy, oak, and sumac, not to mention the blazing sun, long clothing and a wide-brimmed hat is the best protection for your little scout.

Sleeping Outdoors

- Some dads just shove the baby in the sleeping bag with them. But if you actually want to sleep, you might want to make alternate plans. Bring a port-a-crib and you won't have to worry about the baby rolling around your tent.

- Keep a flashlight next to you in your sleeping bag, so you can turn it on as soon as the baby starts to cry. Babies aren't used to the pitch blackness and the spooky sounds of the woods at night, so they get easily rattled.

- A couple of nights before the trip, help the baby get acclimated to outdoor sleeping by staging a dry run with the tent in your backyard.

- Keep in mind that a two-person tent is just not big enough for two adults and a baby. Get a model that accommodates at least three people.

- In cold weather, it's a good idea to dress the baby in the sleep sack wearable blanket.

Take an inflatable baby pool along with you. It has a multitude of uses and deflates to almost nothing. It serves as a:

- Swimming pool

- Bathtub

- Play area

- Diaper changing station

- Impromptu sandbox

Always supervise the baby when he's in the pool, no matter what he's doing.

Waste Disposal

Most state parks have a carry in/carry out policy, which means you can't leave any garbage in the woods. You'll be putting most of it in double-layered plastic bags and hauling it around with you, but what do you do with scat-filled diapers?

The best solution is to bury the scat and then put the diaper in a small plastic bag before putting it into the double-layered bag. When burying scat, you must dig a hole at least 6 inches deep and at least 100 feet from a water source.

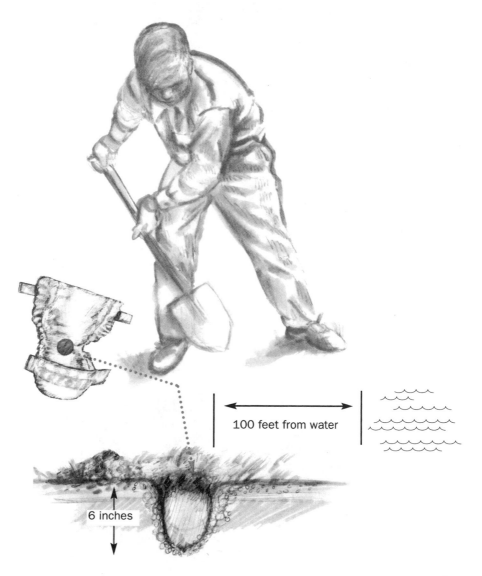

100 feet from water

6 inches

HIKING

The Baby Backpack

Before buying a backpack, bring your baby to the store with you and go on a mini-hike through the aisles with him securely in the pack. If it's not comfortable after five minutes, it certainly won't be comfortable on a three-hour trek through the woods.

Some things to look for in a baby pack:

large removable storage bag for diaper bag items, food, clothing, etc.

removable sun/rain canopy

thickly padded five-point safety harness for baby and expandable child cockpit (not shown)

adjustable padded shoulder straps

sternum strap that clips across your chest to help distribute the weight

wide kickstand for stability when loading and unloading

external easy-access bottle pouch

adjustable padded hip belt

lightweight durable frame (10 lbs. max)

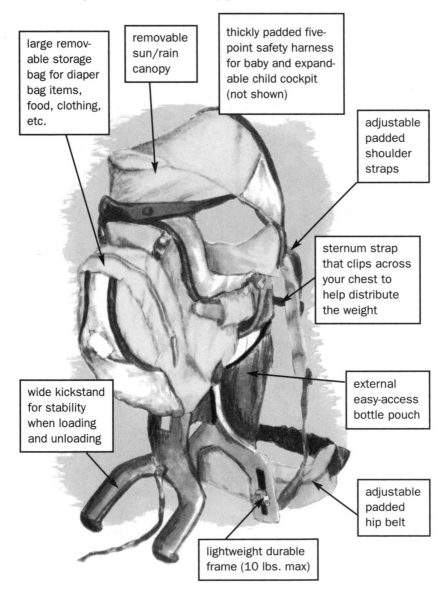

Here Are Seven Things to Consider Before Embarking on a Hike:

1. Never hike alone with your baby. If you happen to twist your ankle, you want another adult to be there.

2. If you are used to carrying around a 60-pound pack, and you have a 20-pound baby, then you should only carry 20 pounds worth of gear. Baby weight is different from gear weight. If you are not careful, the baby's constant shifting can throw you off-balance.

3. Dress your baby more warmly than yourself. Remember that you are moving around while he is basically luggage.

4. The backpack provides your baby a perfect angle to spit up right into your shirt and down your back. It's best not to go hiking right after he's had a big meal, because the jiggling can bring everything up.

5. If it's hot out, give your baby lots of water to keep him hydrated. To cool him off, fill up a spray bottle with lukewarm water and reach back and squirt him once in a while. And if your backpack has a canopy, use it. If not, put a sun hat on him.

6. If you are going to be out for longer than an hour, pack a blanket. Take the baby out of the backpack every once in a while so he can stretch his legs and crawl around on the blanket.

7. Stay on the beaten path, and always stick closely to marked trails, no matter how confident you are in your abilities as a hiker. Having a baby on your back is extreme enough.

H_2O

BEARS AND BABIES

Bears and babies do not mix well, so it would be best to avoid encountering a bear if at all possible. If you are camping anywhere near bear country, you can follow these simple guidelines to avoid a possible confrontation:

Avoid startling a bear.
Most bears will only attack if startled. When walking through the woods, sing loud songs with the baby so that the bears will hear you coming. Clip a baby rattle or loud toy to your belt to add to the noise level.

Keep food and garbage out of reach.
Stow all food, milk, and formula in the trunk of your car or hang it from a tree branch at least ten feet from the ground and four feet out from the tree trunk. It may be a good idea to do this with soiled diapers and other strong-smelling garbage as well.

Keep away from dead things.
When exploring with the baby, never approach a dead animal. It could be a fresh bear kill, and the hunter might be lurking close by.

If you see a bear, make your presence known.
Wave your arms over your head and talk loudly or sing nursery rhymes. You want the bear to register you as quickly as possible, because if he happens to come closer, you don't want to surprise him. Bears don't like surprises.

The First BIRTHDAY PARTY

Your baby will have no memory of his first birthday party, and may not even enjoy it while it's happening. So why go through all the trouble? You can just print the generic birthday party scene from www.beprepared.net, slide a pic of your baby's face in the appropriate space, then scan or photograph the resulting image. Grandma and Grandpa will never know the difference!

But if you choose to actually celebrate:

- Try to keep the party small. A general rule of thumb is that a baby's happiness is inversely proportional to the amount of people in the room with him.

- Don't schedule the party for his regular nap time, thinking that the adrenaline will get him through it. He'll either have a meltdown or sleep through the whole party.

- Don't hire someone to dress up in character for a one-year-old's party. When your baby watches Barney on TV, he's only nine inches tall, and that's a baby's expectation of him. When a six-foot-tall Barney walks into the room, he may incite a Godzilla-like freak-out.

If you've got money to spend, focus your attention on the adult guests. No matter how cute your baby is, they are coming mostly out of obligation, and you want them to know how much you appreciate their presence. Here are various ways to ensure they'll be back for birthday #2:

Gifts

If you don't want extra baby toys littering your house, tell everyone to wrap up boxes that have nothing but tissue paper inside them. Fun for your baby, painless for your friends.

Scheduling

If you want your friends to remain that way, don't schedule the party at the same time as an important sporting event, unless you decide to keep the TV on and make it a sports-themed party. Your baby won't care one way or the other. Just stick a team logo on his pajamas to complete the motif.

Activities

The attention span of a one-year-old will rule out most party games, but if you are looking for something entertaining for the adults to watch, you can stage a Baby Olympics. Compete head-to-head with other dad-baby teams in events such as:

How much frosting can your baby get on his face in under a minute?

How long will your baby keep his party hat on his head before breaking into a wail?

Which baby can crawl across the living room and reach the pile of presents first?

Which dad can make his baby laugh first?

Food

Obviously you need a cake, and sometimes that's all you need. But no matter what time of day it is, provide beer and wine for the adults. It's the least you can do. And before everyone leaves, grab your partner and baby, clink your glasses against your baby's sippy cup, and drink a toast to Toddlerhood.

Life Begins at One

The New Year's PANDA

CONGRATULATIONS!

You've reached the end of your baby's first year (at least in book form). Your accomplishment deserves a reward. In lieu of cash, you are going to receive a powerful fatherhood secret, until now known only to a handful of the most resourceful dads out there. This secret will not only save you thousands of dollars in your lifetime, it will also become a highly anticipated family tradition that can be passed down from generation to generation. And it's called the New Year's Panda.

The New Year's Panda was created because an ingenious dad thought it was unfair that everything went on sale right after Christmas, the day after he needed it. So he started looking for a way to take advantage of the steep post-holiday markdowns and keep his kids happy at the same time. Thus the New Year's Panda was born.

In early December of the following year, the father sat his children down and told them that on New Year's Eve, a large, fuzzy panda visits the homes of children who didn't get what they wanted for the holidays and fills in their wish lists. And to make sure the panda doesn't skip over your house, children need to put some licorice sticks on the front doorstep to make him feel welcome.

Now your baby may be too young to fully comprehend the glory of the New Year's Panda, but it's never too early to start the tradition. If you start now, by the time he's ready for kindergarten it will be an essential part of your family's holiday ritual.

CONCLUSION

The past year seems like a blur, doesn't it? It's almost impossible to remember the time when your big bambino was a newborn and could fit in the crook of your arm. Just a year ago you were holding a squirming bundle of flesh and now you're holding a real live person, who can actually communicate and get around by himself and perform amusing antics.

Not only has the baby grown this past year, but you've grown as well. Do you remember the sheer terror you were feeling the first days home from the hospital? Well, look at you now. You're a seasoned veteran. And we hope you pass on your newfound wisdom to others. When you see a clueless rookie dad in distress, don't snicker at him from afar. Do what you can to lend a hand or offer a word of sage advice. And if you're near a bookstore, why not be a big shot and pick him up his own copy of *Be Prepared*?

We congratulate you on a job well done, and sincerely hope that this year was the best of your life (we already know it was the best year of your baby's life). After what you've been through you deserve some well-earned leave time. But unfortunately, you won't be getting any. Because fatherhood is a 24-7-365 endeavor, and you signed on for the long haul. So hoist up your potty seat and be prepared for year two!

ACKNOWLEDGMENTS

Thanks first and foremost to our editor and friend Rob Weisbach, who championed the book even before it was pitched and has been a constant source of inspiration and great ideas. Grateful acknowledgments go out to all of the other helpful and talented people at Simon & Schuster, especially Bridie Clark, Linda Dingler, Jackie Seow, Aileen Boyle, Alexis Welby, Terra Chalberg, Jim Thiel, Laura Wise, Irene Kheradi, Emily Remes, and John Del Gaizo. Thanks also to our agent, friend, and local baby expert Todd Shuster and everyone at ZSH Literary Agency.

We'd like to thank our parents, Neil and Marlene Greenberg and George and Mary Hayden, for birthing us, feeding us, and babyproofing the stairs. And without your love and support this book could never have happened.

Thanks also to the Be Prepared Research and Development team, headed up by Meg Donaldson, with Jeremy Kareken, Mike Royce, Jon Bines, Kevin Johnson, Herb Emanuelson, Faye Hess, and Jeff Boyd.

Our deepest appreciation goes to our resident pediatricians, Jessica Orbe, M.D., F.A.A.P., and Sarah Baum, M.D., F.A.A.P., who made sure that everything in the book was baby-safe.

And thanks to all of the dads who let us interview, observe, and/or photograph them in action, including Pete Tuneski, Jonathan Stirling, Matt Ahern, John Lewis, Dave Brause, Jon Mysel, Mike Astrachan, Neal Lieberman, Lenny Levy, John Mertens, Paul Flynn, Dave Goldman, Steve Heller, Pablo Martinez, Bob Goetz, Sam Joseph, Andrew Kennedy, Don Hamrahi, Wayne Catan, Howie Allen, Leland Brandt, Joe Badalamente, Jeff Felmus, Todd Hansen, Mike Litsky, Dan Varrichione, Sean Martin Hingston, Rick Winters, David Caminear, Johnny Lampert, John Diresta, Dave Hirsch, Madison Rogers, Tim Mangan, Andrew Tsiouris, Roland Paradis, Mike Rozen, Garrison Schwartz, Ken Friedson, and Charles Bonerbo.

Also, much gratitude to Annabelle Boyd, Marcy Greenberg, Leigh Hayden, Prescott Tuneski, Jeffrey Shaw, Roy and Beth Markham and their New Year's Panda, Eva Hulme, Holley and Russ Flagg,

Lenny and Barbara Grodin, Lucinda Knox, Jodi L. Iannantuono, Elliot and Judy Brause, Lisa Brause, William Stephenson, Ellie and Don Jacobs, Evie Barkin, Joe Clancy, Evan Shweky, Steve Gibbs, Steve Brykman, Raegan McCain, Jon Jacobs, Ellen Lenson, Oona Stern, Monique and Sergio Savarese, Joan Schultz, Adele Phillips, Brian Stern, Chris Mazzilli and the Gotham Comedy Club, Peter Shapiro, Amelia Webster, Derek Lugo, Jude Gallagher, Frank Bozzo, Eva Hulme, Susan and John Javens, Carol Danilowicz, Petra Dielewicz, Rob Carson, Beth and Johnny Garcia and the Manhattan Kids Club, Ilana Ruskay-Kidd and the Manhattan JCC, Suzanne Reiss, Daryle Connors, Stacey Fredericks, Kiki Schaeffer, Matt Strauss, the Sol Goldman YMCA, Schneider's Baby Store, Felina Rakowski-Gallagher and the Upper Breast Side, Mike Abt and Abt Electronics, Derrick Neville and Circuit City, Manny Pagan, Ben Kim, Alexandra Jacobs, Jessica Nooney, Corlette James and everyone at the Small World Preschool, John Rodadero, John and Patty Wrajec, Lillie Rosenthal, the Blodgett family, the Dexter family, the Lamourine family, Dawn Hutchins, Jean DeMerit, Carla Alcabes, Michelle Larrier, Jordan Rubin, Eva Dorsey and Jane's Exchange, Catherine Cetrangolo, Jeffrey Benoit, Alec Lawson, Suzanne Ball, Yvonne Suzuki Licopoli, Jim Mangan, and Peg McCormick.

And most important, we'd like to thank our daughter, Madeline Greenberg, who was a great sport during the nine months we neglected her in order to write a parenting book. Pipsqueak, we could never have been prepared for how much joy you've brought us.

INDEX

ABOUT THE AUTHORS

GARY GREENBERG is the author of the national bestseller *The Pop-Up Book of Phobias* (Rob Weisbach Books), as well as the critically acclaimed *The Pop-Up Book of Nightmares* (St. Martin's Press), and is the coauthor of *Self-Helpless* (Career Press). He is also a comedian and writer and has appeared on Comedy Central and Bravo, as well as numerous national radio networks. He has written material for a number of Comedy Central shows and awards shows and has penned articles for *The New York Times* and *Psychology Today*. He lives in Manhattan with his wife (and collaborator), Jeannie Hayden, and their daughter, Madeline. To learn more about Gary, visit garygreenberg.com.

JEANNIE HAYDEN is an award-winning illustrator and graphic designer whose clients include Nickelodeon, Dialogica, the American Museum of Natural History, *Psychology Today*, the *Village Voice*, L'Oréal, and Liz Claiborne, to name a few. In addition, she illustrated the bestselling reference book *Alternative Medicine* (Future Medicine Publishing) as well as *Self-Helpless* (Career Press). To learn more about Jeannie, visit jeanniehayden.com.